JOHN
CALVIN

JOHN CALVIN

Sally Stepanek

1987
CHELSEA HOUSE PUBLISHERS
NEW YORK
NEW HAVEN   PHILADELPHIA

EDITORIAL DIRECTOR: Nancy Toff
SENIOR EDITOR: John W. Selfridge
ASSOCIATE EDITOR: Marian W. Taylor
MANAGING EDITOR: Karyn Gullen Browne
COPY CHIEF: Perry King
EDITORIAL STAFF: Maria Behan, Karen Dreste,
            Pierre Hauser, Kathleen McDermott,
            Howard Ratner, Alma Rodriguez-Sokol,
            Bert Yaeger
PICTURE EDITOR: Elizabeth Terhune
PICTURE RESEARCH: Tamara Fulop
ART DIRECTOR: Giannella Garrett
LAYOUT: Irene Friedman
ART ASSISTANTS: Noreen Lamb, Carol McDougall,
            Victoria Tomaselli
COVER ILLUSTRATION: Richard Leonard

Frontispiece courtesy of The Bettmann Archive

First Printing

Library of Congress Cataloging in Publication Data

Stepanek, Sally. JOHN CALVIN.

(World leaders past & present)
Bibliography: p.
Includes index.
1. Calvin, Jean, 1509–1564—Juvenile literature.
2. Reformation—Biography—Juvenile literature.
I. Title. II. Series.
BX9418.S78   1986   284'.2'0924 [B] 85-26915

ISBN 0-87754-515-4

Contents

CHELSEA HOUSE PUBLISHERS

WORLD LEADERS PAST & PRESENT

ON LEADERSHIP
Arthur M. Schlesinger, jr.

LEADERSHIP, it may be said, is really what makes the world go round. Love no doubt smooths the passage; but love is a private transaction between consenting adults. Leadership is a public transaction with history. The idea of leadership affirms the capacity of individuals to move, inspire, and mobilize masses of people so that they act together in pursuit of an end. Sometimes leadership serves good purposes, sometimes bad; but whether the end is benign or evil, great leaders are those men and women who leave their personal stamp on history.

Now, the very concept of leadership implies the proposition that individuals can make a difference. This proposition has never been universally accepted. From classical times to the present day, eminent thinkers have regarded individuals as no more than the agents and pawns of larger forces, whether the gods and goddesses of the ancient world or, in the modern era, race, class, nation, the dialectic, the will of the people, the spirit of the times, history itself. Against such forces, the individual dwindles into insignificance.

So contends the thesis of historical determinism. Tolstoy's great novel *War and Peace* offers a famous statement of the case. Why, Tolstoy asked, did millions of men in the Napoleonic wars, denying their human feelings and their common sense, move back and forth across Europe slaughtering their fellows? "The war," Tolstoy answered, "was bound to happen simply because it was bound to happen." All prior history predetermined it. As for leaders, they, Tolstoy said, "are but the labels that serve to give a name to an end and, like labels, they have the least possible connection with the event." The greater the leader, "the more conspicuous the inevitability and the predestination of every act he commits." The leader, said Tolstoy, is "the slave of history."

Determinism takes many forms. Marxism is the determinism of class. Nazism the determinism of race. But the idea of men and women as the slaves of history runs athwart the deepest human instincts. Rigid determinism abolishes the idea of human freedom—

the assumption of free choice that underlies every move we make, every word we speak, every thought we think. It abolishes the idea of human responsibility, since it is manifestly unfair to reward or punish people for actions that are by definition beyond their control. No one can live consistently by any deterministic creed. The Marxist states prove this themselves by their extreme susceptibility to the cult of leadership.

More than that, history refutes the idea that individuals make no difference. In December 1931 a British politician crossing Park Avenue in New York City between 76th and 77th Streets around 10:30 P.M. looked in the wrong direction and was knocked down by an automobile—a moment, he later recalled, of a man aghast, a world aglare: "I do not understand why I was not broken like an eggshell or squashed like a gooseberry." Fourteen months later an American politician, sitting in an open car in Miami, Florida, was fired on by an assassin; the man beside him was hit. Those who believe that individuals make no difference to history might well ponder whether the next two decades would have been the same had Mario Constasino's car killed Winston Churchill in 1931 and Giuseppe Zangara's bullet killed Franklin Roosevelt in 1933. Suppose, in addition, that Adolf Hitler had been killed in the street fighting during the Munich *Putsch* of 1923 and that Lenin had died of typhus during World War I. What would the 20th century be like now?

For better or for worse, individuals do make a difference. "The notion that a people can run itself and its affairs anonymously," wrote the philosopher William James, "is now well known to be the silliest of absurdities. Mankind does nothing save through initiatives on the part of inventors, great or small, and imitation by the rest of us—these are the sole factors in human progress. Individuals of genius show the way, and set the patterns, which common people then adopt and follow."

Leadership, James suggests, means leadership in thought as well as in action. In the long run, leaders in thought may well make the greater difference to the world. But, as Woodrow Wilson once said, "Those only are leaders of men, in the general eye, who lead in action. . . . It is at their hands that new thought gets its translation into the crude language of deeds." Leaders in thought often invent in solitude and obscurity, leaving to later generations the tasks of imitation. Leaders in action—the leaders portrayed in this series—have to be effective in their own time.

And they cannot be effective by themselves. They must act in response to the rhythms of their age. Their genius must be adapted, in a phrase of William James's, "to the receptivities of the moment." Leaders are useless without followers. "There goes the mob," said the French politician hearing a clamor in the streets. "I am their leader. I must follow them." Great leaders turn the inchoate emotions of the mob to purposes of their own. They seize on the opportunities of their time, the hopes, fears, frustrations, crises, potentialities. They succeed when events have prepared the way for them, when the community is awaiting to be aroused, when they can provide the clarifying and organizing ideas. Leadership ignites the circuit between the individual and the mass and thereby alters history.

It may alter history for better or for worse. Leaders have been responsible for the most extravagant follies and most monstrous crimes that have beset suffering humanity. They have also been vital in such gains as humanity has made in individual freedom, religious and racial tolerance, social justice and respect for human rights.

There is no sure way to tell in advance who is going to lead for good and who for evil. But a glance at the gallery of men and women in *World Leaders—Past and Present* suggests some useful tests.

One test is this: do leaders lead by force or by persuasion? By command or by consent? Through most of history leadership was exercised by the divine right of authority. The duty of followers was to defer and to obey. "Theirs not to reason why,/ Theirs but to do and die." On occasion, as with the so-called "enlightened despots" of the 18th century in Europe, absolutist leadership was animated by humane purposes. More often, absolutism nourished the passion for domination, land, gold and conquest and resulted in tyranny.

The great revolution of modern times has been the revolution of equality. The idea that all people should be equal in their legal condition has undermined the old structure of authority, hierarchy and deference. The revolution of equality has had two contrary effects on the nature of leadership. For equality, as Alexis de Tocqueville pointed out in his great study *Democracy in America,* might mean equality in servitude as well as equality in freedom.

"I know of only two methods of establishing equality in the political world," Tocqueville wrote. "Rights must be given to every citizen, or none at all to anyone . . . save one, who is the master of all." There was no middle ground "between the sovereignty of all and the absolute power of one man." In his astonishing prediction of 20th-century totalitarian dictatorship, Tocqueville explained how the revolution of equality could lead to the *"Führerprinzip"* and more terrible absolutism than the world had ever known.

But when rights are given to every citizen and the sovereignty of all is established, the problem of leadership takes a new form, becomes more exacting than ever before. It is easy to issue commands and enforce them by the rope and the stake, the concentration camp and the *gulag*. It is much harder to use argument and achievement to overcome opposition and win consent. The Founding Fathers of the United States understood the difficulty. They believed that history had given them the opportunity to decide, as Alexander Hamilton wrote in the first Federalist Paper, whether men are indeed capable of basing government on "reflection and choice, or whether they are forever destined to depend . . . on accident and force."

Government by reflection and choice called for a new style of leadership and a new quality of followership. It required leaders to be responsive to popular concerns, and it required followers to be active and informed participants in the process. Democracy does not eliminate emotion from politics; sometimes it fosters demagoguery; but it is confident that, as the greatest of democratic leaders put it, you cannot fool all of the people all of the time. It measures leadership by results and retires those who overreach or falter or fail.

It is true that in the long run despots are measured by results too. But they can postpone the day of judgment, sometimes indefinitely, and in the meantime they can do infinite harm. It is also true that democracy is no guarantee of virtue and intelligence in government, for the voice of the people is not necessarily the voice of God. But democracy, by assuring the right of opposition, offers built-in resistance to the evils inherent in absolutism. As the theologian Reinhold Niebuhr summed it up, "Man's capacity for justice makes democracy possible, but man's inclination to injustice makes democracy necessary."

A second test for leadership is the end for which power is sought. When leaders have as their goal the supremacy of a master race or the promotion of totalitarian revolution or the acquisition and exploitation of colonies or the protection of greed and privilege or the preservation of personal power, it is likely that their leadership will do little to advance the cause of humanity. When their goal is the abolition of slavery, the liberation of women, the enlargement of opportunity for the poor and powerless, the extension of equal rights to racial minorities, the defense of the freedoms of expression and opposition, it is likely that their leadership will increase the sum of human liberty and welfare.

Leaders have done great harm to the world. They have also conferred great benefits. You will find both sorts in this series. Even "good" leaders must be regarded with a certain wariness. Leaders are not demigods; they put on their trousers one leg after another just like ordinary mortals. No leader is infallible, and every leader needs to be reminded of this at regular intervals. Irreverence irritates leaders but is their salvation. Unquestioning submission corrupts leaders and demands followers. Making a cult of a leader is always a mistake. Fortunately hero worship generates its own antidote. "Every hero," said Emerson, "becomes a bore at last."

The signal benefit the great leaders confer is to embolden the rest of us to live according to our own best selves, to be active, insistent, and resolute in affirming our own sense of things. For great leaders attest to the reality of human freedom against the supposed inevitabilities of history. And they attest to the wisdom and power that may lie within the most unlikely of us, which is why Abraham Lincoln remains the supreme example of great leadership. A great leader, said Emerson, exhibits new possibilities to all humanity. "We feed on genius. . . . Great men exist that there may be greater men."

Great leaders, in short, justify themselves by emancipating and empowering their followers. So humanity struggles to master its destiny, remembering with Alexis de Tocqueville: "It is true that around every man a fatal circle is traced beyond which he cannot pass; but within the wide verge of that circle he is powerful and free; as it is with man, so with communities."

—*New York*

1

A New Generation

On November 1, 1533, the entire theology faculty of the Sorbonne, the most important college of the University of Paris in France and a bastion of Roman Catholic orthodoxy, gathered in the Church of the Mathurins in Paris to hear Nicolaus Cop, the newly elected rector of the university, give his inaugural address. In a remote corner of the church, sitting apart from the distinguished professors, cardinals, bishops, and monks, a 24-year-old student named John Calvin anxiously waited for the sermon to begin. He had helped write it.

Cop approached the lectern and began to read in clear, forceful Latin. To those assembled, the words had an almost rebellious tone. "As Erasmus — and other notable theologians — have shown in their commentaries on the Bible," the rector declared, "*all* men are sons of God! Let us plead to Christ, who is the true and *only* mediator with God. It is *only* the doctrine of Christ that we should follow." The congregation shifted nervously in their pews.

As the speech continued, many in the audience started to jeer at the rector, calling him a heretic, or dissenter from established Church doctrine.

> *Nothing less than to create in man a new nature was Calvin's far-reaching aim, to regenerate character, to simplify and consolidate religious faith.*
> —JOHN MORLEY
> British historian

Martin Luther (far left) and Desiderius Erasmus (center), two great thinkers of the Reformation and Renaissance. The 16th century brought tremendous expansion in science, arts, and letters, with a new emphasis on human values and the importance of reason.

Martin Luther nailed his 95 "theses" (complaints against the Catholic church) to the door of the castle church at Wittenberg in 1517, beginning the movement known as the Reformation. Sixteen years later, Calvin risked death by openly supporting Luther's ideas.

14

Schweinitz

Pabst Leo X.

These Catholic scholars were being confronted with a renunciation of standard church teachings, and the author of the piece was obviously sympathetic toward Protestantism. This new, non-Catholic form of Christianity was based upon the teachings of the German religious reformer Martin Luther, who had been condemned as a heretic by Pope Leo X in 1521. In asserting in the sermon that all men were equal before God, Cop was denying the authority of the pope; in declaring that Jesus Christ (whom Christians believe to be God's only son) was the only true mediator with God, he was questioning the validity of such Catholic rituals as worshiping at saints' shrines and confessing one's sins to a priest.

As soon as the rector had finished his address, the professors rose abruptly and stormed out of the building. Cop hurriedly descended from the pulpit, donned his cloak, and left the church by a side door. Calvin, who had begun to realize the enormity of the risk he had taken in assisting Cop with his speech, was almost paralyzed by fear. Many of the leaders of the religious reform movement that had grown up in Germany in the wake of Luther's initial assault on the Church had already been put to death for their beliefs. Calvin recognized that the Catholic authorities in France would look no more kindly upon heretics than had their counterparts in Germany. "Does anyone know that I, too, was responsible for the sermon?" he wondered, as he trudged home through the deep November snow to his rooms in the Collège du Fortet.

Later that night, Calvin went to visit Cop. But when he arrived at the rector's rooms in the Collège de Sainte-Barbe, he found them deserted. When he visited the college again the next morning, he found that his friend's bed had not been slept in. "Has Nicolaus been arrested?" he wondered. "Has he deserted me? Will I be accused of heresy?" Nervous and afraid, Calvin hurried back to the Collège du Fortet, desperately hoping that he and Nicolaus might be afforded some protection by the fact that Nicolaus's father, Guillaume Cop, was personal physician to the French king, Francis I.

Shortly after Calvin returned home, he heard a

knock at the door. "I have a message from Nicolaus Cop," a voice said. The door opened a crack. "You are John Calvin, are you not?" the messenger cautiously asked.

"Yes, I am John Calvin. What do you want?"

"Master Cop bids me tell you that he has fled the city. You must do the same."

Calvin was stunned. He realized that Cop would never have abandoned his teaching post and the rectorship unless he knew himself to be in grave

Pope Leo X was a member of the extravagant and ruthless de' Medici family from Renaissance Florence. Elected in 1513, Leo was determined to preserve all the wealth and power of the Roman Catholic church. Luther was so great a threat to the security of the Church that Leo excommunicated him in 1520.

danger. The messenger continued, "You must go to your friend the Erasmian," he announced. "Nicolaus said you would understand."

Calvin discarded his student's cap and gown, packed his few belongings, and tiptoed down the dark, narrow hallway that led from his room to the college courtyard. Once through the gates, he looked back to make sure that no one was following him, and sped away into the night. A few hours later, when Calvin was already several miles south of Paris, his rooms were raided by representatives of the Paris Parlement, the most important of France's high courts of justice, which wielded political power second only to the king. His books, lecture notes, and correspondence were seized, and 50 of his associates arrested. A reward was offered for information as to the whereabouts of Nicolaus Cop.

This would not be the last time Calvin was forced to flee for his life. In a land where Catholicism was the state religion and the king was pledged to its defense, there were few places where a young theologian whose ideas were even slightly influenced by Protestant teachings could secure a sympathetic hearing.

Eventually, John Calvin would emerge as one of Protestantism's foremost theologians. He would become one of the most important figures of the period of religious, political, and social upheaval known as the Reformation, which began in 1517, when Luther first posted his famous *Ninety-five Theses*, or propositions for debate, in which he spoke out against the questionable practices to which the Roman Catholic church was then resorting in its quest for wealth. And Calvin's life and work cannot be properly understood unless one knows something of Luther, the condition of the Roman Catholic church in the early 16th century, and the events of the first decade of the Reformation.

At that time, Christianity had a widespread intellectual and spiritual influence in Europe. The Roman Catholic church was the sole authority in all matters dealing with the Christian faith, and it was also the wealthiest and most powerful institution in Europe. The Church owned almost one-third of all the land in the Holy Roman Empire, a vast tract of territory covering much of present-day Austria, Belgium, Czechoslovakia, West Germany, eastern France, the Netherlands, and northern Italy.

In some areas, one-fourth of all business property was held by the Church. The Church imposed an annual levy, known as "Peter's Pence," on every household in Christendom. In addition to this tax, every Catholic was supposed to pay the Church a tithe, a tax amounting to 10 percent of his or her income. Tithes were used to support the local parish church. The revenues from these sources had made the Church extremely rich. With power and prosperity, however, came decadence and disrepute.

Many Catholics had become disturbed by the avarice and immorality of the popes, cardinals, and other high-ranking churchmen. Ecclesiastical appointments were often sold for huge amounts of

Papal indulgences are bought and sold at a country fair. Luther was horrified by this practice, which swelled church coffers with money given by gullible peasants, who believed they were buying a better afterlife. Luther believed that salvation was between the individual and God alone.

money. Some clergymen would buy numerous offices and thus control vast revenues. Many bishops were also princes, and cardinals enjoyed the same position as princes in the social hierarchy. Some senior churchmen held several sees, or regional appointments, yet failed to perform their duties in any of them. Several popes of the 15th and 16th centuries were notorious for their corruption.

Many of the pontiffs of Luther and Calvin's time sent armies into battle, hunted game, and generally neglected their religious duties in favor of worldly pleasures. Alexander VI, who reigned from 1492 to 1503, was a spectacularly immoral pontiff. Leo X, who reigned from 1513 to 1521, spent more money on parades and gambling than he did on either the Church or the arts. In criticizing the papacy, Luther criticized an institution that possessed very little of the moral and spiritual authority that it had known several centuries earlier.

Faced with this situation, many people had begun to feel that the Church was in need of reform. Previous would-be reformers, however, had met with fierce opposition from the religious establishment. Only a strong, charismatic leader with a large following could hope to succeed. And it was just such a leader that Luther proved to be.

One of the forms of ecclesiastical avarice that Luther attacked with particular vehemence during his earliest years as a reformer was the practice of selling indulgences — letters issued by the pope that purported to guarantee the forgiveness of sins. The fact that the Church was capitalizing on the gullibility of faithful Christians disturbed Luther.

An indulgence was basically a transfer of credit. At that time, the Church taught that Jesus Christ, the Virgin Mary (Christ's mother), and all the saints were better than they needed to be to earn spiritual salvation. The excess of merit that these holy figures had acquired was regarded as infinite in the case of Christ, whom Catholics believe to be both God and the son of God, and entirely without sin. These excess merits were viewed as a kind of treasury that could be drawn upon by sinners so as to improve their spiritual "solvency."

The selling of indulgences had become especially widespread after 1476, when Pope Sixtus IV announced that indulgences could shorten the amount of time that a sinner would have to spend in purgatory — the place of punishment where, according to Catholic doctrine, the dead make atonement for all their sins. This particular papal pronouncement had encouraged believers to purchase indulgences both for themselves (to shorten their future sentences) and for their deceased loved ones. Many of the letters of indulgence issued by Sixtus's successors had promised complete forgiveness of sins rather than merely a reduction in the penalty for having committed them.

Luther's assault on Catholic doctrine had its origins in the revolutionary conclusions regarding the nature of faith that he reached while studying St. Paul's Letter to the Romans. The 17th verse of the first chapter reads, "For therein is the righteousness of God revealed from faith to faith: as it is written, the just shall live by faith." Luther's reading of this text convinced him that Christians did not have to try harder and harder, through good deeds and self-sacrifice, to live a perfect life. Luther came to believe that "the righteousness of God is that by which the righteous live through a gift of God, namely by faith." Luther had previously hated the phrase "righteousness of God" because he felt that such a notion implied that God was a remote and heartless punisher of the sinful.

The implications of Luther's revelation — which was the turning point of his life and of the history of Christianity — are summed up as follows by historian John M. Todd in his book *Luther: A Life*: "[Luther now believed that man] was always a sinner but always justified — if only he turned to Christ. It was the way of *sola fides*, faith alone, which he found through *Scriptura sola*, only through the words of Scripture, and not through [ecclesiastical] law or conventions. . . . All fear was banished in the certainty of grace. No longer was it a matter of an assent to certain doctrines, but a simple personal act of surrender, a total trust in God known in the Word, his son, Jesus [Christ]."

> *The early sixteenth century saw great changes in architectural style as the need for defense passed; the introduction of gunpowder revolutionized war and the printing press threw open the doors of knowledge; the horizon itself expanded dramatically as sea-discoverers went to new worlds. But the farmer, the peasant, the artisan, the housewife, and the child all went about their tasks in pretty much the same way their distant forebears had done.*
> —T. H. L. PARKER
> British historian

Martin Luther, as painted by Lucas Cranach the Elder. The famous German artist was friendly with Luther and illustrated some of his writings. Cranach was the first great Lutheran painter, and his altarpieces can still be seen today in some German churches.

In 1520 Luther completed and published the three treatises that are now considered to have been the cornerstone of the Reformation. Many of the issues that he dealt with in these treatises were later to concern Calvin.

In the treatise entitled *To the Christian Nobility of the German Nation Concerning the Reform of the Christian Estate*, Luther criticized many traditional Catholic rituals, the pride and selfishness of the Catholic clergy, and the doctrine that held that the pope's interpretation of the Bible was both correct and not to be disputed. He voiced his disapproval of the fact that, under Church doctrine, priests enjoyed preferment over ordinary believers; that is, the clergy was seen as more worthy of salvation. Luther also denounced the institution of priestly celibacy, which forbade priests to marry.

The second of the three treatises, *Prelude on the Babylonian Captivity of the Church*, was addressed to scholars, theologians, and the clergy. In this tract, Luther criticized many of the rituals of the ceremony known as the Mass, as well as the entire system of sacraments — the various rites and practices of the Church. Luther's attack on the sacramental system was so uncompromising that, upon reading it, the Dutch scholar and theologian Erasmus declared, "The breach is irreparable." Historian Roland H. Bainton has explained Erasmus's reaction thus: "The reason was that the pretensions of the Roman Catholic church rest so completely upon the sacraments as the exclusive channels of grace and upon the prerogatives of the clergy, by whom the sacraments are exclusively administered. If sacramentalism is undercut, then [dependency on the priesthood] is bound to fall."

There were seven sacraments: marriage; ordination; extreme unction (the Catholic practice of anointing a dying person with oil); confirmation; penance; communion (or the Eucharist); and baptism. Luther, believing that the only true sacraments were those that constituted external signs of a solely Christian *and* Christ-instituted grace, acknowledged only two — baptism and communion (which the reformers called the Lord's Supper). Lu-

The Roman church, once the holiest of all, has become the most licentious den of thieves, the most shameless of all brothels, the kingdom of sin, death, and hell. It is so bad that even Antichrist himself, if he should come, could think of nothing to add to its wickedness.
—MARTIN LUTHER
in an open letter to Pope
Leo X, September 6, 1520

ther firmly believed that the other five sacraments were false inasmuch as they had been prescribed by the papacy, an institution that he considered human and historical rather than divine.

One of the most controversial elements of this treatise was Luther's rejection of transubstantiation, the miracle that, according to Catholic doctrine, occurs when the priest administers the sacred bread and wine during communion. For Luther, the bread and wine dispensed to communicants by the priest were not, as Catholics still believe, the actual flesh and blood of Christ. Luther denied that any such miracle could be performed by the word of man. He was convinced that the priest, in administering the Eucharist, does not *make* God. However, because the precedent for the Lord's Supper was Christ's "Last Supper," the meal that he took with his disciples before he died and at which he declared the bread and wine to be his body and

"To the Christian Nobility of the German Nation Concerning the Reform of the Christian Estate" **was the title of Martin Luther's first pamphlet, published in 1520. This revolutionary document attacked the privileges of priests, criticized their rule of celibacy, and challenged the pope's infallibility.**

An den Christli
chen Adel deüt
scher Nation.
von des Christ
lichen standes
besserunng D.
Martinus
Luther
Wittenberg.

THE BETTMANN ARCHIVE

Erasmus, the great Dutch humanist, was an early supporter of the Reformation. He wrote several satirical works on Catholicism, and collected 3,000 proverbs of classical Greek and Roman authors. Erasmus was the first to realize that the ideas of Luther would irrevocably divide the Christian faith.

blood, Luther believed the Lord's Supper to be of paramount sacramental value. He viewed it as a ritual of communion with God and Jesus Christ, and, equally important, as a rite of fellowship with other Christian believers.

Related to Luther's assault on several of the sacraments was his declaration that all believers were priests. "Not only are we most free kings of all," he wrote, "but we are priests forever, by which priesthood we can appear before God, pray for one another and teach one another." Luther argued that Christians both could and should be responsible for their own spiritual well-being: "All Christians possess a truly spiritual status and among them there is no distinction save that of function. This is so because we possess one baptism, one faith, one gospel, and are equal as Christians. Anyone who has emerged from the waters of baptism may pride himself on

A dying man is anointed with oil as he receives the last sacrament. Luther disapproved of this Catholic practice, believing that it had not been ordained by Jesus Christ. For him the only valid sacraments for Christians were baptism and communion.

already being ordained priest, bishop, or pope, although not everyone may be suited to exercise such an office. Therefore let every congregation elect a devout citizen to be their priest."

In the third treatise Luther set forth the essence of his understanding of the Christian life. Entitled *The Freedom of a Christian Man*, the work began with a seemingly paradoxical assertion, taken from St. Paul's writings in the New Testament, regarding the nature of Christian freedom, "A Christian is a free lord of all, subject to none. A Christian is a dutiful servant, subject to all."

More clearly stated, the Christian act, by definition, is an act of compassion and brotherly love. Such an act is never simply a mere following of rules or adherence to a body of laws, but is rather an expression of deep faith in God. According to Luther, the Christian is most free because he or she acts from the heart and does so without regard for the dictates of others. Consequently, the Christian is also obliged to act out of unqualified and unconditional love.

Another important element of Luther's thought (and one that was greatly to preoccupy Calvin) was his belief that the Church had forsaken its original purity and, consequently, any supportable claim to authority, as far back in history as the 8th century. It was at this time, Luther believed, that the papacy had first begun to acquire an appetite for temporal power — an appetite, as it turned out, that could only be satisfied at the expense of spirituality.

Luther was essentially a religious conservative. His proposals for reform were intended to achieve a *renewal* of the Church. He wanted to recreate the Church as it had been when the writings of St. Augustine, a 5th-century Christian theologian, had informed its nature, or, even more ideally, as it had been during the first five centuries of its existence — solidly based upon the Gospels and the teachings of St. Paul, an apostle of the 1st century who helped spread Christianity to much of the Roman Empire.

The German reformer had begun a movement that would spread throughout many of the nations of Europe, including Calvin's homeland. And the controversy and conflict that had been triggered by Luther's teachings would continue long after the great reformer's death.

When Luther made the first public declaration of his revolutionary beliefs in 1517, Calvin was only eight years old. At the beginning of the 16th century, France was a strong, peaceful, and prosperous nation of 15 million people. Although the economies of several other European nations had been weakened by the influx of gold and silver into Spain from the New World, France remained largely unaffected by these developments.

It was also at the beginning of the 16th century that French art, architecture, scholarship, social conventions, and even French Catholicism had begun to be transformed by the ideals generated during the cultural period known as the Renaissance. (This is a French term that means rebirth.) The Renaissance, which originated in Italy, was characterized by a revival of interest in the literature, philosophy, and politics of ancient Greece and

Title page of the first complete German Bible, published in 1534. Luther had translated the New Testament in one year while in hiding as a refugee. He wanted the Scriptures to be read and understood by all.

A monk with a paunch, drawn by German artist Hans Holbein the Younger, illustrated Erasmus's satire *In Praise of Folly*. Reformers often portrayed corrupt clergy, accusing them indirectly of mortal sin. The monk's gluttony could even represent the greed of the papal court in Rome, which Luther so fiercely attacked.

Rome. The Renaissance gave rise to several new forms of consciousness, one of which came to be known as humanism.

Developed independently of Catholic teachings by Italian intellectuals during the 14th and 15th centuries, humanism was eventually to influence all Europe. Its adherents viewed the world in strictly human terms. Humanism represented a radical departure from medieval ways of thinking, which had viewed the world exclusively in relation to God.

The relationship between the humanists and the Church was sometimes uneasy. Many churchmen distrusted the humanists because they concerned themselves with the study of pre-Christian, pagan cultures. However, despite the fact that humanism and Catholicism were essentially incompatible, there was to be no open conflict between them. This was mainly because the popes assumed a leading role as patrons of the new learning.

The ruler of 16th-century France, King Francis I, was an immensely powerful sovereign. One of the most important sources of his strength was the agreement known as the Concordat of Bologna, which he concluded with Pope Leo X in 1516. The Concordat helped maintain the Gallican (French) church's traditional partial independence from Rome, and, at the same time, made that institution essentially subordinate to the monarchy.

Under the terms of the Concordat, the pope remained fully entitled to receive *annates* (a tax paid to the papacy by new ecclesiastical appointees) from French churchmen, while Francis gained the right to nominate the high dignitaries of the Roman Catholic church in France.

This alliance between the papacy and the French monarchy proved profitable to both parties. It also meant that Francis and his successors had a much stronger incentive to effect the suppression of Protestantism than did most of Europe's Catholic princes, many of whom enjoyed no such mutually advantageous arrangements with the Church.

Scholars are still uncertain as to whether the Reformation was brought to France from Germany or whether an indigenous reform movement was already at work in France when Luther came to prominence. Guillaume Briçonnet, bishop of Meaux, is known to have endeavored to enhance the quality of spiritual life in his diocese by ordering copies of humanist scholar and theologian Jacques Lefèvre d'Étaples's French translation of the New Testament to be distributed free to the poor. Lefèvre was the most famous member of the group of deeply religious humanists that Briçonnet had gathered at his court. Lefèvre was greatly influenced by the writings of French theologian Jean Gerson, who held that the spiritual meaning of the biblical text was its literal meaning as understood with the aid of the

Calvin was a man of order and peace born into a world of conflict. A conservative by nature, by upbringing, by conviction, his ideas became among the most revolutionary in Europe. The Calvinist church, aristocratic in tendency, which he prized and which he devoted his life to establishing, became one of the platforms for democracy in succeeding centuries.
—T. H. L. PARKER
British historian

Holy Spirit. This approach to biblical interpretation characterized both Luther's and Lefèvre's works. In a book that he published in 1505, Lefèvre — expounding on a theme that would later be echoed by Luther — asserted that Scripture should be the only authority for men's statements about God. He also held, like Luther, that salvation is a gift from God, and that one cannot attain salvation through good works, but only by faith.

Lefèvre and the other French reformers of his generation were not as radical as the reformers in Germany. Many of their philosophical and theological innovations had more to do with their humanism than with any deep-seated hostility toward the Church. The historian Lewis W. Spitz writes in *The Protestant Reformation, 1517–1559* that the French reformers' "mystical piety and Christian humanism could easily be accommodated within the bounds of tradition . . . they remained good Catholics to the end. They were religious renovators rather than theological revolutionaries in the Protestant sense."

Although its beginnings are difficult to place, the French Protestant Reformation was certainly in progress as Calvin was coming of age. However, French Protestantism still lacked a systematic theology. It was to be Calvin who would devote much of his life to attempting to remedy this situation by developing and setting down what Spitz describes as "the most complete systematic theology produced by a major reformer." (A similar task had already been performed by German classical scholar and reforming theologian Philipp Melanchthon, who was one of Luther's closest colleagues. In his *Theological Commonplaces*, which was published in 1521, Melanchthon had managed to reduce Luther's varied writings to a systematic statement.)

As the Reformation progressed, major differences concerning matters of doctrine would divide the Lutherans and the second generation of Protestant reformers. Calvin would emerge as the most important theologian of this new generation, addressing many of the questions that Luther had raised but did not live to answer.

King Francis I of France reigned from 1515 to his death in 1547. To increase his own power, he signed a treaty with Pope Leo X that allowed Francis to appoint all French church dignitaries. With the king politically bound to Rome, Lutheran reformers in France would suffer great difficulty and increasing danger.

As the young Calvin fled Paris at the messenger's bidding, he was haunted by the realization that he might yet be burned at the stake as a heretic. He reproached himself for having dared to help Cop write such a provocative and inflammatory sermon. And yet he believed that he had no choice but to speak out and defy the teachings of the Church. Of his feelings at this time, Calvin later wrote, "Unless I opposed them to the utmost of my ability, my silence could not be vindicated from the charge of cowardice and treachery!"

Such were the beginnings of Calvin's defiance of Catholicism, a defiance to which, within two years of his flight from Paris, he would give expression in his *Institutes of the Christian Religion* — the definitive statement of the Protestant Reformation and one of the greatest theological treatises ever written.

2

The Young Student

Near the northern French city of Noyon, boatmen passed the banks of the city listening to the daily chiming bells of many monasteries and churches. The people of Noyon often remarked that in their city "no one could speak three words without being interrupted by a bell."

Surrounded by the echoing chimes of the city, Jeanne le Franc of Cambray gave birth to her second son, Jean Cauvin, later known as John Calvin, on July 10, 1509. Three years later Jeanne died, leaving her husband Gérard with three sons — Charles, John, and the young Antoine. Gérard eventually married again and had two daughters.

Calvin had very little recollection of his mother. He did remember, though, that when he was three his mother lifted him in her arms so that he could touch a holy relic — a fragment of the skull of St. Anne, mother of the Virgin Mary. Jeanne was a deeply religious person, as were many of the citizens of Calvin's homeland. He later recalled being led by his mother through church processions and feasts, delighted by the glow of the candles, the haunting faces of the statues, and the excited ringing of the

> *I am merely a man from among the common people.*
> —JOHN CALVIN

John Calvin was to be the most powerful voice of the Reformation's second generation. Some of his ideas would be far more extreme than Luther's. His early yearnings, however, were for knowledge and scholarship rather than faith.

bells. Young Calvin was surrounded by the overwhelming presence of the Catholic church — its rituals, doctrines, and unquestioning obedience to the pope. He knew the Catholic Mass by heart from a very young age, having recited the *Pater Noster* (Our Father) and *Ave Maria* (Hail Mary) from memory perhaps thousands of times.

Noyon has a long history of political and ecclesiastical importance. In the mid-8th century, Charlemagne, who founded the imperial Carolingian dynasty, and his brother, Carloman, were crowned joint kings of the Franks in Noyon. Two centuries later, Hugh Capet, the first king of the long-reigning Capetian dynasty, was also crowned in this city. For over 1,000 years Noyon had also been the seat, or center of power, of the bishop who dominated all aspects of local life in the region. At Calvin's birth, the ruling bishop was Charles de Hangest.

To Calvin's good fortune, his father Gérard eventually became the secretary to Bishop de Hangest. Gérard was a well-respected attorney, or *promoteur*, in Noyon, and was often enlisted to counsel the town's clergy. He was also the town registrar and the fiscal agent for the county. Gérard, therefore, was part of both the legal and Church communities. Having come from a family of lowly artisans and boatmen, Gérard's climb to his position of secretary to the bishop was quite remarkable.

Gérard's association with Bishop de Hangest enabled young Calvin to be granted a "benefice," an appointment as chaplain in the little chapel of La Gésine in Noyon Cathedral on May 21, 1521. On the eve of *Corpus Christi*, a Catholic festival day of parades, Calvin donned a black robe and stood before the bishop. He held a lighted candle in his right hand and knelt to repeat the bishop's prayer. The bishop then cut five locks of hair from Calvin's head. This formed a "tonsure," or crown of hair, which symbolized Calvin's call to the ministry. As the choir sang, Calvin presented his candle to the bishop, who offered a blessing. Thus the small boy of 12 became a member of the Catholic clergy. Calvin received a salary of three measures of corn from the neighboring county of Voienne and the wheat harvest of 20 grain fields at Espeville. In later years Calvin would add the pastorate of Saint-Martin de Martheville and the curacy of Pont l'Évêque to his clerical responsibilities.

Calvin spent many hours with the de Hangest family in Noyon, especially with Charles's two young nephews, Joachim and Ives, as well as their cousin, Claude. He rode their beautiful horses and played games in the fields and gardens of the de Hangest mansion — so different from his small home near the corn market in the center of town. Here the young Calvin participated in the aristocratic ways of the rich, and sampled the tastes and lifestyle of the French leisure class, the impressions of which would remain with him for the rest of his life.

Calvin received his basic schooling at the Collège des Capettes, a small boys' school — only eight students — at which he was an outstanding student. The institute was named for its students' *capettes*,

Charlemagne forces the pagan Saxons to accept baptism in the Christian faith. The French king's first coronation was held in 768 at Noyon, where Calvin was born more than seven centuries later. Charlemagne was crowned as the first Holy Roman emperor in 800 and used his military might to spread the influence of Roman Catholicism throughout much of Europe.

This image of St. Anthony of Padua shows his tonsure, or crown of hair. For centuries this was the symbol of Catholic clergymen. At the age of 12, Calvin was ceremonially given a tonsure after his father secured him a position as chaplain at the local parish church.

hooded capes in which the professors routinely placed lists of Latin vocabulary words to be memorized for upcoming lessons. The school was located opposite St. Maurice Church on the road to Pont l'Évêque. There Calvin was educated in the humanities as well as falconry and horsemanship.

In 1523, two years after Calvin's appointment as chaplain, the bubonic plague struck Noyon and hundreds were dying. At the same time, the Flemish to the north were battling for their independence from Spain. Many citizens of Noyon, fearing both the plague and raids for plunder by the Spanish soldiers passing through France en route to Flanders, were escaping to safety.

Gérard could not leave Noyon, but he planned for Calvin to escape and continue his studies in Paris. Although young Calvin had to leave his school and family behind, the canons, or officials of the cathedral, permitted him to maintain his chaplaincy and he was granted "liberty to go wherever he pleased during the plague, without loss of his allowance."

Accompanied by the three de Hangest boys, Calvin mounted a heavily laden mule and set off southwest on a 60-mile journey along the Oise River to Paris. Calvin, now 14, looked forward to the culture, excitement, and fine schooling of the country's largest city. A canon of Noyon would later write of Calvin, "Thus flying from the pestilence, he went to catch it elsewhere." To be sure, Paris would hold many new things for the young man from Noyon.

Gérard was planning a career in the clergy for his son. He dreamed that Calvin would get his degree in the arts, then in divinity, then go on to become a famous cardinal. Calvin passed by the windmills and vast farmlands of the flat northern countryside. He had many days to think about his future life in Paris. The boys finally entered the city in August 1523, and made their way through the narrow and crowded streets.

They crossed the bridge over the Seine and arrived on the Left Bank, the intellectual center of Paris. Here Calvin began his studies at the Collège de la Marche of the University of Paris. The boys registered at the college, Joachim and Ives proudly an-

> *It is easy to perceive something divine in the sacred Scriptures which far surpasses the highest attainments and ornaments of human industry.*
> —JOHN CALVIN

nouncing themselves as nephews of the bishop of Noyon. Calvin introduced himself as Johannes Calvinius, in order to sound like a Latin scholar.

Soon after, Calvin bid farewell to his friends, who left for their lodgings on the rue St. Jacques. Calvin guided his mule back over the bridge to a small locksmith's shop near the chapel of St. Germain-l'Auxerrois. Here his Uncle Richard, a Parisian locksmith, furnished him with a small room in his attic. The leaky ceiling and drafty windows did not discourage him; Calvin stayed up very late into the night, as was his custom, to read and study, even though classes were to begin very early the next morning.

Life was very difficult at the college, especially for a boy of 14. Calvin attended Mass before dawn at the chapel next to his uncle's house, then crossed the Seine River and climbed the hill to the school. The college was a dark and dirty building. The students were often whipped for the slightest offense, and they cared little for their studies.

Calvin's studies, however, were of the utmost importance to him. He never missed a lecture — although he was known to fall asleep at his desk because of the late hours he kept studying. He diligently studied French, Latin, logic, and the works of the great theologians and humanists, especially the Christian philosopher St. Augustine, who is known for his two great works, *Confessions* and *The City of God.* Calvin also studied the works of Thomas Aquinas, particularly his *Summa Theologica (Compendium of Theology)*; Jacques Lefèvre d'Étaples, the French humanist scholar; and, of course, he immersed himself in the Bible.

Calvin's Latin instructor, Mathurin Cordier, a former priest, was a powerful influence on the young scholar. Calvin later dedicated a commentary to Cordier, and would eventually invite him to teach in his own academy. Calvin once told his teacher, "When my father sent me, still only a boy, to Paris . . . Providence so ordered that for a short time I had the privilege of having you as my teacher, so that I might be taught by you the true method of learning." Cordier, at 46, was a veteran teacher and

"Doctor Beak of Rome" is the satirical name of this plague physician in protective clothing. His "beak" is filled with pleasing smells, and with his rod he advises on treatment from a safe distance. Fear of the plague forced Calvin's father to send the young boy away to school in Paris in 1523.

had seen many fine pupils in his classrooms, but few like Calvin. The two formed a deep friendship that lasted for many years.

Calvin often discussed the recent religious writings of the day with Master Cordier and his fellow students. One friend, a distant cousin of Calvin's named Pierre Robert, nicknamed "Olivétan," often talked with Calvin about the notorious "heretic," Martin Luther.

Olivétan informed Calvin that Luther's teachings centered on faith and that the monk's desire to reform the Catholic church came from Jacques Lefèvre. This must have startled Calvin for Lefèvre was a professor at the university, and recently Master Cordier had predicted that Calvin would become the next Lefèvre. Olivétan also taught Calvin of the writ-

St. Thomas Aquinas was the most important philosopher and theologian in the Roman Catholic church in the 13th century. He defined the relationship between faith and reason, saying that reason could operate independently within a context of faith. Calvin read his most famous works while studying theology in Paris.

ings of Erasmus, particularly his *In Praise of Folly*. Calvin was amused by the philosopher's satirical descriptions of priests, popes, and the false rituals of the Catholics, but wondered what the clergy of his university would do if they found this blasphemous book in a student's possession.

Calvin soon left Master Cordier, Olivétan, and the de Hangest boys to enroll in another school at the university in 1526 — the Collège de Montaigu. This had been the school of Erasmus and the French writer François Rabelais. Calvin's new college, how-

Aristotle was one of the greatest philosophers and scientists of classical Greece. He formed the basis for logical thought and influenced 16th-century humanist philosophy. His ideas were an essential part of Calvin's early studies.

ever, was hardly worthy of its famous graduates. Erasmus described the school in sordid detail: "Thirty years ago I was at a college in Paris, where you swallowed so much theology that the walls were impregnated with it; but I took nothing else of it away with me than a cold disposition and a number of vermin. The beds were so hard, the food so wretched, the sitting up and studying at night so difficult, that in the first year of their stay in that college many men of great promise became bandy-legged, blind, or leprous, if they did not die. Some

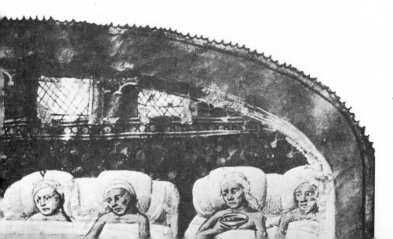

A hospital for plague victims. In the 14th century the dreadful disease wiped out over one-quarter of Europe's population.

bedrooms, near which were the privies, were so dirty and infected that nobody who had slept in them came out alive or without the germ of some terrible sickness. The punishments consisted in flagellations, which were dealt with a severity that can only be expected from a hangman!" Rabelais, years later, described the lice crawling on the walls. The school was the oldest and dirtiest in Paris. Prostitutes strolled by its gates at the top of the nearby hill.

Life was very severe for Calvin at the Collège de Montaigu. He rose at 4:00 A.M., had lessons until 6:00, and heard Mass, conducted in Latin. The students attended lectures and discussions until lunch at 11:00 A.M. From noon until 2:00 P.M. they took examinations, and from 3:00 to 5:00 had more lessons, followed by prayers in chapel. After dinner the students organized for debates, took another exam — and were in bed by 8:00 or 9:00.

Calvin studied under some of the leading scholars in Paris. One in particular was Noël Béda, the head of the college and a notorious persecutor of Lutheran heretics. Calvin's philosophy courses covered such thinkers as Aristotle, Thomas à Kempis, John Duns Scotus, and William of Ockham. The lessons taught at the academy were very conservative; there was little room in lectures to entertain the new ideas from Germany. Calvin continued to read Luther's works, however, and discussed the new reforms with his good friend Nicolaus Cop, the young son of the king's physician. Cop strongly believed that Luther was weeding out the corruption in the Church. Although it was dangerous to agree with the new Protestant doctrines, Calvin soon began to agree with Cop on many points.

The French Lutherans met with increasing danger from persecution while Calvin was at college, but they persevered because they had a royal ally in the king's sister, Marguerite of Angoulême, queen of Navarre. She was a proponent of the Reformation and had continually pleaded the case of the French Lutherans to her brother, King Francis I. Unfortunately, however, by 1525 the royal family was no longer in France. The Holy Roman Empire was fighting France for possession of territories in northern

A priest in fool's garb addresses a dull and stupid congregation. This illustration by the German artist Hans Holbein the Younger appeared in Erasmus's *In Praise of Folly,* much to the delight of the book's author. Calvin first read the controversial book in secret, after being introduced to it by a fellow student.

Italy and eastern France. At the Battle of Pavia, near Milan, Francis had suffered defeat by the forces of Emperor Charles V, and was taken prisoner and sentenced to confinement in Madrid, Spain. Queen Claude of France had died only days after Francis had left for battle. Alone in the tower of Alcazar, Francis longed for comfort and companionship. Marguerite left the endangered French Protestants to be with her brother. Consequently, the students whispered quietly when discussing Luther; they never knew who might be listening. While the royal family was detained, the faculty blacklisted Luther's writings and dismissed the reformist Lefèvre from the Sorbonne. In 1525 they publicly burned his

THE BETTMANN ARCHIVE

François Rabelais wrote entertaining and satirical novels that are still enjoyed today. Originally a Catholic, he later adopted some of the Lutheran beliefs. A former student at the college Calvin attended, he was as appalled by its miserable conditions as was Calvin.

Charles V, the Holy Roman emperor, is shown returning from battle with troops. He wished to preserve the Holy Roman Empire against the forces of Protestantism, and fought for years with France over disputed territory. In 1525 he held Francis I prisoner in Spain.

translation of the New Testament. Paris was in a religious turmoil.

For five years Calvin read the classics of theology and philosophy by day; by night he studied the writings of the reformers. Although he received his master of arts in 1528, he would not complete the program at Montaigu. Sometime between 1525 and 1528, Calvin received a letter from his father directing him to leave the university. Gérard had be-

come disenchanted with the clergy and decided that his son would be better off practicing law.

Perhaps it was after this sudden change that Calvin began to question God's role in his life. Was his future already planned for him? Must he follow the wishes of his father — or was he free to make his own decisions and determine his destiny? What was the role of his own free will in guiding the course of his life?

3

New Destinations

Gérard was not only thinking of his son when he transferred Calvin to the University of Orléans to study law. Gérard had fallen out of favor with the clerics of Noyon because of business disagreements — and was subsequently excommunicated from the Church. Gérard would not have his son a clergyman in its services. Besides, a legal career for his son was quite appealing.

Arriving at Orléans in March 1528, Calvin discovered that his cousin Olivétan had already been studying there for a year. In the liberal city of Orléans, 70 miles southwest of Paris, Olivétan could freely discuss the Reformation without the threat of exile or death. Calvin heard his friend reading aloud the translations of Luther's writings made by one of Jacques Lefèvre's pupils, Louis de Berquin.

One day in April 1529 Olivétan burst into Calvin's study. De Berquin had been burned at the stake! News of the French Parlement's recent purge of Protestants quickly spread to the southern liberals. Many Lutherans were being killed — but de Ber-

There is a universal call by which God, through the external preaching of the word, invites all men alike. Besides this there is a special call which, for the most part, God bestows on believers only.
—JOHN CALVIN

John Calvin left Paris in 1528 to study law in accordance with his business-minded father's wishes. But he continued to read philosophy in Orléans, and to discuss Reformation ideas with fellow students.

THE BETTMANN ARCHIVE

An unchaste monk is thrown into the Tiber (the river that divides Rome) by two devils. Many anticlerical cartoons of Calvin's period portrayed Church officials as hypocritical traitors to their vows.

quin's death was particularly shocking for he had been a favorite of Marguerite of Angoulême. Now no one was safe.

Olivétan fled to Strasbourg, Germany, to join Lefèvre, leaving Calvin behind to ponder all that he had taught him and to tend to his legal studies. Calvin was an outstanding student, and often served as an instructor when professors were absent. He studied the *Corpus juris civilis*, a codex of civil law compiled under the Roman Emperor Justinian, and the jurist Gratian's *Decretum*, the basis of canon, or church, law. He continued to read the ancient Greek Stoic philosophers, the Roman philosopher Seneca, and particularly Augustine, who would have a tremendous influence on his own writing. In an effort to better his studies, Calvin left Orléans in the autumn of 1529 to study under the brilliant Italian scholar Andrea Alciati at Bourges. Although Calvin received his law degree that same year, a legal career still did not appeal to him.

On May 26, 1531, Calvin received news of his father's death. Gérard, having been excommunicated by the Church, died a condemned man and therefore could not be buried in hallowed ground. Calvin, not wanting his father buried under the gallows of Noyon where the condemned were laid to rest, returned to Noyon. After much pleading with the bishop, Calvin had his father buried next to the Noyon cathedral. Despite his deep sadness at the loss of his father, Calvin felt liberated. He was now free to give up his legal career and return to Paris to follow his true calling. Reasoning that God's wishes determined the course of his life, Calvin journeyed back to Paris.

Paris was once again safe for the reformers. King Francis I had returned to his capital in March 1526, after being forced to sign a degrading treaty with the Holy Roman emperor. The French king seemed to have had a change of heart toward Protestantism during his incarceration. In reality, Francis's renewed tolerance of the Lutherans was purely political. His archenemy, Holy Roman Emperor Charles V, was battling the German Protestant princes. To spite his foe, King Francis professed tolerance for

the Lutherans. To rebuke the Sorbonne, Francis exiled its dean, Noël Béda, who had condemned the king's sister for her Protestant beliefs, and he invited Lefèvre back into France to tutor his sons. The French Protestants were not entirely convinced that they were safe in his kingdom, however, and the secretive meetings continued.

Calvin arrived in Paris in June 1531, and lodged in the Collège du Fortet. His secluded room faced the old convent of the Bernardines on the upper end of the rue des Sept-Voies. His friends, on hearing reports from Orléans of Calvin's fine reputation as a humanist scholar, encouraged him to write his own commentaries.

Calvin began to write a humanist commentary on the 1st-century Roman philosopher Seneca's work *De clementia (On Clemency)*. Scholars trace many of Calvin's later theories to those of Seneca. Calvin's first work, published in 1532, therefore, was very important.

King Francis I returns to France in 1526 after being released from captivity by Charles V. Though the French provinces demanded by Charles remained loyal to the French king, Francis never regained full power. He obeyed the Holy Roman emperor only under pressure, and, to spite his foe, he was as tolerant as possible of the French reformers. But Calvin dared not trust the king's newfound goodwill.

Portrait of Charles V, who reigned as Holy Roman emperor during the intense early stages of the Reformation. He was struggling against the German Protestant princes when Francis was released, and the French king joined the German nobles' cause as far as he could. Charles eventually had to abdicate all his titles.

Seneca declared that all governments must submit to a divine guiding will. Calvin commented that "this is also the teaching of our religion, that there is no power but of God and that everything is ordered by him." In reading Seneca, Calvin began to consider his many questions about the role of God in the affairs of life, the Church, and the state.

Although Calvin was most concerned with theological issues, or questions about God, he approached Seneca from a humanist perspective. He cited only three quotations from the Bible, while he referred repeatedly to Erasmus and Augustine. While Calvin's perspective would later change, the format for his future writings is found in his commentary on *De clementia*. In it he used a particular "exegetical" approach, which would influence many writers to come. "Exegesis," derived from a Greek word which means "to guide," refers to any interpretation of a word or passage, particularly one from the Bible. In studying Seneca's grammar and examining parallel passages, Calvin laid the foundation for future "hermeneutic" studies, or studies of the methods and principles used in the interpretation of religious works.

Many of the professors in Paris used Calvin's first commentary in their classrooms and Calvin even persuaded a friend to advertise the book from a church pulpit. He also sent a copy to Erasmus, who inspired the work. Although he was only 23 years old, Calvin gathered quite a following. Theodore Beza, a pupil of Calvin's and a respected poet and historian, reported from Paris that "a few months' residence here made him known to all who desired a reform in religion." Yet Calvin still had profound doubts as to his true calling. He continued to read Luther and the reformers, developing their ideas with his own classical background.

The time would soon come when Paris was no longer the haven of free thinking and debate. Calvin's future would not be found behind the conservative walls of the university; the faculty there would violently reject his liberal ways and he would leave Paris once again in search of his true destiny.

> *I may truly name this book the anatomy of all parts of the soul; for no one can feel a movement of the spirit which is not reflected in this mirror. All the sorrows, troubles, fears, doubts, hopes, pains, perplexities, stormy outbreaks, by which the souls of men are tossed, are depicted here to the very life.*
> —JOHN CALVIN
> writing about the Book of Psalms

4

The Fight Begins

In his *Commentaries* Calvin explains that "whilst my one great object was to live in seclusion without being known, God so led me about through different turnings and changes that he never permitted me to rest in any place, until, in spite of my natural disposition, he brought me forth to public notice." Calvin's life would be one of constant travel, debate, and discouragement. He would indeed be thrust into the public arena, but not through his humanist commentary on Seneca.

Calvin often spent time with his good friend, Nicolaus Cop. Through contacts of his influential father, Cop learned that the French Parlement was planning to condemn Marguerite of Angoulême as a heretic and burn her at the stake if she returned to France. She had written an extremely controversial book based on the teachings of Luther, *The Mirror of a Sinful Soul*. The book was an imaginary dialogue between Marguerite and a young girl in heaven. The Sorbonne firmly opposed the book and called upon the Parlement to condemn her as a heretic. The prospect of losing their protector deeply upset reformers throughout France.

> *First I was devoted to this superstition of Papism so obstinately that it was not easy to draw myself out of this abyss. But by a sudden turning God subdued my heart to obedience.*
> —JOHN CALVIN

A Reformation preacher. The austere simplicity seen in this engraving was identified with Reformation thought. Sometime around 1533 Calvin experienced a religious conversion, and with a total trust in God, he yielded his own reason to a higher will. As little as he wanted the limelight, he felt called to preach the Reformation faith.

A monk and a nun are shown profaning their holy vows of chastity. As Calvin was refining his religious ideas, corrupt Catholic clergy continued to figure in satirical Reformation art, and the rift between Catholics and Protestants widened.

Cop developed a plan that was made possible by the authoritative gap left open by Noël Béda's exile. The faculties of medicine and art awarded Cop the rectorship of the Sorbonne for one year. As rector, Cop was to give the sermon on All Saints' Day. He chose to use this opportunity to defend the doctrines of true spirituality. Cop gained Calvin's assistance for this project.

The two men worked for days on the address. On November 1, 1533, the faculties assembled in the Church of the Mathurins. From his place in the back of the church, Calvin could hardly see his friend at the pulpit, but he knew every word of the sermon — here was a phrase from Luther, there an idea from Erasmus. Certainly the faculty was not expecting the words of the reformers.

As soon as the rector finished, the scholars hurried from the church, exchanging threats of expulsion, excommunication, and worse. Calvin would not see his friend again for quite some time. Aware of the great danger they had provoked, Cop fled the country, leaving only a message of warning for his friend. The purge had begun. Francis I would no longer tolerate the heretical Lutherans.

Perhaps it was at this time that Calvin wrote, "Like a flash of light, I realized in what an abyss of errors, in what chaos I was!" Although the exact date is still open to conjecture, Calvin had indeed experienced a "conversion." His turning was not so much a conversion to believe; he had already confessed Jesus as his Savior. His revelation was probably more of a decision to turn away from humanism toward a total commitment to and trust in the will of God, the God who had an intimate tie with the daily course of life — as Calvin later described, the God who "foresees all things."

Calvin described the experience as a turn to godliness: "God by a sudden conversion subdued and brought my mind to a teachable frame, which was more hardened in such matters than might have been expected from one at my early period of life. Having thus received some taste and knowledge of true godliness, I was immediately inflamed with so intense a desire to make progress therein that although I did not altogether leave off other studies, I yet pursued them with less ardor." The conversion of Calvin is somewhat ambiguous, but it was after this time that he began to formulate the doctrine that would become the handbook of the reformist theology.

Calvin assumed the name "Charles d'Espeville" when he escaped from Paris and the condemnation of the Sorbonne faculty. He journeyed through the valleys of Touraine and the wooded plains of Poitou to Angoulême and the home of his friend Louis du Tillet, the curé, or parish priest, of Claix and canon of Angoulême.

Du Tillet welcomed his friend into his mansion and led him to a table spread with wine and meats. He explained that it was his son, Abel, who had informed Cop of the Parlement's plans. As registrar for the Parlement, Abel overheard that they had immediately convicted Cop without a trial and were

> *He did not immediately understand the whole ecclesiastical implications of his new faith; he did not forthwith cut himself off from all associations with the Church of his youth. All that happened was that his mind, willful in its submission to authorities, accepted now the sole authority of God.*
> —T. H. L. PARKER
> British historian,
> describing Calvin's conversion

The troubled Catholic church pitches and tosses in a sea of discontent. Reformers within and outside the Catholic faith endangered Rome's wealth and power. Calvin's austere religion represented a very real threat to the wealthiest institution in all of Europe.

planning to use him, the son of the king's physician, as an example to the other Lutherans in France. King Francis had agreed to the sentence.

Calvin's escape to Angoulême was remarkably fortunate. In du Tillet's mansion he found a large library where he read nothing but the Bible and began to outline his ideas concerning God's nature and the importance of faith, the Bible, and obedience. "If a believer's eyes are turned to the power of the resurrection," Calvin considered, "in their hearts the cross of Christ will at last triumph over the flesh and sin."

Calvin heard that Jacques Lefèvre was staying at the exiled Marguerite of Angoulême's home in Nérac, the capital of the French Navarre. He set off to visit the aging scholar, who was now 78 years old. The old man had seen much despair through the trials of the Reformation — his translation was condemned, his student de Berquin was burned at the stake, and he himself was no longer safe in Paris. The two reformers had much to discuss.

Calvin excitedly told Lefèvre about his new ideas for the reformation of the church. Upon hearing

THE BETTMANN ARCHIVE

The first queen to rule England alone, Mary Tudor was called "Bloody Mary" because of her ruthless persecution of Protestants and other heretics. Her reign of terror in England was to embody all that Calvin and his sympathizers feared would happen in France.

Calvin's intentions, Lefèvre warned the young reformer to be moderate. In the many ordeals to come, Calvin would remember, though not always heed, Lefèvre's advice.

The old scholar quietly whispered to Calvin as he was leaving, "You have been chosen, my son, as a mighty instrument of the Lord, through whom God will erect his kingdom in France." The young Calvin could hardly imagine himself returning to the dangers of his homeland, let alone erecting a kingdom there. Before he left, Lefèvre suggested that Calvin journey to Paris to see a cloth merchant named Estienne de la Forge. He wrote a letter of introduction and recommendation for Calvin, and sent him on his way to Paris.

5

Back to the Homeland

Before Calvin traveled to Paris, he had to tend to some important business in his hometown of Noyon. The cathedral canons were still paying him for his benefice as curate at Pont l'Évêque. He could no longer accept the payments for a job that he failed to perform.

Calvin's resignation from his post of curate was more than an act of conscience. He was formally breaking with the Catholic church. On May 4, 1534, as he walked toward the cathedral and his old home, he considered the seriousness of what he was about to do. The cathedral canons were still angry with his father; perhaps Calvin would be arrested upon his resignation — or even worse. His older brother Charles was still serving as curé in Noyon; perhaps Charles could protect him.

With Charles at his side, Calvin met with the new notary in the cathedral and formally signed his dismissal. The following day, the canon of Cambray, a friend of the family, was ordered to confront Charles to determine whether he, too, was a heretic. On the eve of Trinity Sunday, the brothers staged a demonstration in the cathedral against the canons. Officials, bearing weapons, arrested Calvin and his brother and escorted them to the dark, damp prison of Corbaut Gate in Noyon.

We are subject to the men who rule over us, but subject only in the Lord. If they command anything against Him, let us not pay the least regard to it.
—JOHN CALVIN

Calvin at work in his study. The radical theologian realized that his new mission was to communicate his faith in a systematic manner, thus giving Protestantism the structure he felt it lacked. Imprisonment and danger only deepened his conviction that God Himself had called him to this important task.

Prelu Ascesiana

French Reformation literature was printed on small
presses like this one. Estienne de la Forge, at whose
house in Paris Calvin lived in
1534, paid for French versions of the Bible to be pri-
vately printed and then distributed. But these small
circulations of documents
were not enough to unify the
splitting Protestant factions.

*I have not so great a struggle
with my vices, great and
numerous as they are, as I
have with my impatience. My
efforts are not absolutely
useless; yet I have never been
able to conquer this
ferocious wild beast.*
—JOHN CALVIN

Charles was released after several days, but Calvin
was detained until September. While in jail, Calvin
began to realize, as he would later write, that his
"very being is nothing else than subsistence in God
alone." Imprisonment, persecution, even estrange-
ment from his family and friends would be the price
he was willing to pay to reform the Church and be
obedient to the will of God. Nothing else mattered
to him. Calvin did not question his jail sentence nor
the many trials to come: "Anyone who has been
taught by Christ's lips that all the hairs of his head
are numbered . . . will consider all events are governed by God's secret plan."

Once out of jail, Calvin followed Lefèvre's sugges-
tion and called upon Estienne de la Forge in Paris.
The merchant was "a rich and God-fearing man"
whose deep faith inspired the young reformer. Estienne used his great income for printing and dis-
tributing the French Bible, together with short
Bible commentaries. Calvin soon became a member
of de la Forge's large family.

Calvin preached every week in the merchant's
crowded basement on rue St. Martin. The family
could not tell their Catholic neighbors that they

were housing a Lutheran preacher nor holding secret meetings, so Calvin was supposedly teaching Latin to their children.

In the evening, Catholics sympathetic to the reformers gathered to dine at de la Forge's large table. The guests discussed the increasingly turbulent situation in Europe. Wars had broken out in Switzerland between Catholic and Protestant cities. The Catholic towns of Fribourg and Lucerne were battling the Protestant districts of Bern, Zurich, and Basel.

Reports were also coming in from Paris of scandalous practices in the reformed churches. Many of Luther's adherents were misinterpreting his doctrine of Christian "liberty." There was also much dissension among Protestant factions. Lacking a centralized church, the Reformation was growing weaker and more corrupt. The Lutheran Christians needed a guide, a uniform doctrine that would unite them in the many countries in Europe and lead the people ignited by Luther's dwindling flame.

By the early winter of 1534, Paris was becoming too dangerous for Calvin to remain. A new purge had begun as a result of the Affair of the Placards. Lutherans were placing placards, or posters, in Paris, Orléans, and Tours. They called the pope, cardinals, bishops, and priests "liars and children of Satan." They also denounced the Catholic Mass, causing great anger among the clergy. The crude

All I had in mind was to hand on some rudiments by which anyone who was troubled with an interest in religion might be formed to true godliness. I labored at the task for our own Frenchmen in particular, for I saw that many were hungering and thirsting after Christ and yet that only a very few had even the slightest knowledge of Him.
—JOHN CALVIN
on his reasons for writing
the *Institutes of the Christian Religion,* 1536

German artist Albrecht Dürer drew this famous image of "the Bible in the hands of every man." Without printing, Reformation ideas could not have achieved their widespread influence. Now every man could read the Bible in his own language or Latin, and no one who could read had to depend on the Church for instruction.

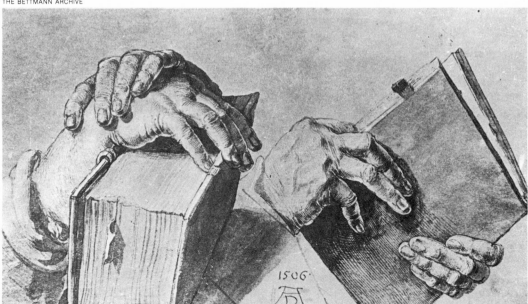

"The Explanation of the Monk-Calf," reads this anticlerical cartoon from Luther's time. The monk is shown as half-animal, and looks much more interested in earthbound matters than in higher achievements.

notices provoked a renewed Catholic fervor to silence the heretical Lutherans.

Francis I was especially enraged. On October 13 the king had been hunting near his château at Amboise when, during the night, someone broke into the royal chambers. In the morning the king awoke to find a placard on his bedroom door. He immediately put to death the palace guard responsible for the breach in security.

With lighted candles, Francis led a solemn march of his court and clergy to the cathedral of Nôtre Dame in Paris. He then captured and imprisoned hundreds of Protestants — burning 35 at the stake, Calvin's brother Charles included.

De la Forge urged Calvin to flee before it was too

late. Calvin's dear friend would himself be condemned as a heretic and killed at the stake, and his wife, Charlotte, would spend many years in prison.

Calvin escaped to the safety of du Tillet's mansion in Angoulême. On his journey, Calvin had an idea. He was familiar with a book by Erasmus entitled *Institutio Principis Christiani*, a book of instruction for a Christian prince. What the Protestants needed, he decided, was instruction. He would write a Protestant guide, a manual of doctrine for the dispersed believers. He would title it after Erasmus's book, calling it *Institutio Christianae Religionis*, or *Institutes of the Christian Religion*.

In his book, Calvin planned to examine and develop the doctrines of faith that Luther outlined. Someone had to lead the people; too many had died misunderstanding the Gospel. Calvin's journey to Angoulême was a difficult one. Surprised by his own decision to leave the home of his youth, Calvin wrote to a friend, "I have learned from experience that we cannot see very far before us. When I promised myself an easy, tranquil life, what I least expected was at hand."

Purges of French Protestants (Huguenots) began in earnest in 1534 after anti-Catholic placards appeared in streets and on buildings. Calvin fled Paris to avoid the persecution. Brutality and violence were evident on both sides of the struggle, and continued to erupt for the next two centuries.

6

The Sword of the Word

France had become a land plagued by fear and persecution. By 1534 King Francis had become completely intolerant of the French Protestants. Every corner of the country was being searched for those even remotely connected with the new theology. Even the printer of Marguerite's book was put to death. If Calvin and du Tillet were discovered in their Angoulême hideaway, they would certainly be burned at the stake. The two reformers decided that they must flee the country as soon as possible.

Du Tillet and Calvin traveled east to the Protestant city of Basel, Switzerland. This city was the home of Erasmus, Olivétan, who had just completed a French translation of the Bible, and Nicolaus Cop, whom Calvin had not seen since the sermon on All Saints' Day.

Finally, Calvin was in a city that welcomed Protestants. Basel, with its many students, writers, and preachers, was a lively city in 16th-century Switzerland. Located on the Rhine River, Basel was an important trade center. It had the only university in the country, and printers, bookbinders, and philosophers, as well as artists, were plentiful.

> *All our wisdom, insofar as it really deserves the name wisdom and is sure and reliable, comprises two basic things—the knowledge of God and the knowledge of ourselves.*
> —JOHN CALVIN
> the introductory sentence of the *Institutes*

A saint preaches to his devoted followers. In spite of the spread of printing and literature, word of the Reformation reached most converts by mouth. Only the educated could read the Bible for themselves, and Calvin used his own powerful personality to convince many followers.

Under the assumed name Martinus Lucanius — a homage to Martin Luther — Calvin lodged in the home of a widow. He began writing what would turn out to be the most important work of the Protestant Reformation — the *Institutes*.

Institutio Christianae Religionis was only the beginning of the title of Calvin's theological treatise. The entire title was: *The Institutes of the Christian Religion, containing the whole sum of piety and whatever it is necessary to know in the doctrine of salvation. A work very well worth reading by all persons zealous for piety, and lately published. A preface to the most Christian king of France, in which this book is presented to him as a confession*

John Duns Scotus was a famous Scottish medieval philosopher and theologian. Calvin drew on Scotus's writings to understand how God could be directly experienced by the most faithful believers.

THE BETTMANN ARCHIVE

of faith. Author, John Calvin of Noyon. Basel, MDXXXVI.

Calvin wanted to present "a small treatise containing a summary of the principal truths of the Christian religion . . . published with no other design than that men might know what was the faith held by those whom I saw basely and wickedly defamed." In dedicating the work to the king, Calvin also wanted to demonstrate that the reformed church was not a subversive organization — Francis's court need not fear an overthrow of the government by Protestants.

Calvin echoed St. Augustine's teachings in asserting that a king is actually an instrument of God and should serve in God's name. In turn, the people were not to rebel against the civil government, but obey it. The spiritual government of God reigns within Christians; God had given them a civil government to rule the world of external affairs.

The first edition of the *Institutes* was written in Latin and published in 1536. It had 520 pages and was small enough to be carried in a pocket, allowing the reader to have access to it at all times. Originally, Calvin followed the order of Luther's "catechism" by only constructing six chapters. However, over the course of 24 years Calvin added another 74 chapters to this original plan, revising and expanding his ideas. In all versions, he never retracted a statement about the character of the Church, the nature of the state, or the nature of God. By the final edition of 1559, the *Institutes* comprised four books of 80 chapters. The first 18 chapters discussed "knowledge of God, the Creator." The next 17 addressed "the knowledge of God, the Redeemer in Christ." In the following 25 chapters Calvin presented "the notion of divine grace, and the benefits of the effects which follow from it." The last 20 chapters contained a discussion of "the eternal means or aids by which God calls us into communion with Christ and retains us in it."

Calvin did not wholly originate many of the basic concepts in his work. He made good use of ideas set forth by earlier theologians and philosophers. For instance, one main tenet of Calvinist doctrine

> *God, who is perfect righteousness, cannot love the iniquity which He sees in all. All of us, therefore, have that within us which deserves the hatred of God.*
> —JOHN CALVIN
> in the *Institutes*

stemmed from a 5th-century debate between St. Augustine and a philosopher named Pelagius. The scholarly argument concerned the question of original sin: is a human born already damned, corrupted by the sin of Adam and Eve in the garden of Eden? Or had Adam's transgression, or sin, merely set a bad example? Pelagius argued the latter position — that humanity has seen the bad example of Adam, but an individual is born without a sinful nature. He concluded that one is able to exercise one's own free will to believe and obey God totally.

In contrast, Augustine asserted that human nature had been completely perverted by Adam's original fall, and that no one could know or obey God. Augustine also postulated that divine grace alone can save. Grace is God's unmerited favor, his divine assistance, which saves men and women from the punishment of sin. But although God offers this grace to all, God predestines some to eternal life, planning that some would be saved even before the earth was created. According to Augustine, people do not have a free will to choose God for themselves. Their will is enslaved by sin.

Like Augustine, Martin Luther emphasized salvation by grace alone, and believed that the human will is bound by sin and cannot freely choose God. (He entitled one of his chief works *The Bondage of the Will.*) Basically all of the early reformers agreed that one is helpless in sin and God saves souls by grace alone; people cannot earn their salvation by good works or sacrifice. The debate, however, was on the nature of this choice of salvation. Is God the actual author of faith? Does God predestine some to salvation and others to damnation? Must one rely utterly on God for all things, or can a person exercise one's own will — especially one's will to believe?

One point in particular runs throughout Calvin's work, especially in the later editions: only God saves sinners; because they are sinners, people cannot save themselves. Calvin explains the idea of predestination through a logical progression of scriptural principles. He describes human nature as utterly separated from God: "Let us hold this as an undoubted truth which no siege engines can shake:

St. Augustine in his chambers. His most famous work, *The City of God*, confessed a belief in predestination and integrated New Testament ideas with classical Greek philosophy. Calvin echoed the saint's belief that civil government was an extension of God's will and that Christians should obey both.

the mind of man has been so completely estranged from God's righteousness that it conceives, desires, and undertakes only that which is impious, perverted, foul, impure, and infamous. The heart is so steeped in the poison of sin, that it can breathe out nothing but a loathsome stench. But if some men occasionally make a show of good, their minds nevertheless ever remain enveloped in hypocrisy and deceitful craft, and their hearts bound by inner perversity." Calvin thus paints a gloomy picture of humanity without God.

There is hope, however, for the person who responds to God's love and forgiveness. According to Calvin, even though men are so desperately lost in

69

The torments of hell as depicted by Dutch painter Dirck Bouts. Calvin believed that all men are sinners, and without God's intervention are condemned to hell. The idea that sinners are predestined by God to damnation or salvation was fundamental to his theology.

King Edward VI of England was Henry VIII's only legitimate son. He was intensely devoted to the Protestant faith (Anglicanism) his father had founded in England. Calvin dedicated two commentaries to Edward, and wrote instructions to the young king's regent on how best to reform the English church.

sin they can begin to respond to God's love because God is sovereign; and they are saved as a result of God's choice. God chooses the sinner, the sinner does not choose God. In the 1539 edition of the *Institutes* Calvin states that "it must first of all be understood that some are predestined to salvation and others to damnation. Then it must be explained that the world is governed by the providence of God, meaning that whatever happens must depend upon His discretion." Calvinism is often mistakenly associated solely with this concept of predestination. Actually, Calvin saw the doctrine only in the greater principle of God's ultimate sovereignty. For Calvin, people are totally dependent on God.

Calvin's teachings may be summarized in what have been called "the five points of Calvinism." These points were established in a meeting of Catholic church members, called a "synod," that met in the city of Dort, Holland, in 1618, to discuss various religious schools challenging Calvin. They outlined the teachings of the *Institutes* in five statements: 1. Human nature is totally depraved and unable to freely choose God; 2. God unconditionally "elects" some to be saved; 3. Christ died for the elect only and offers them the gift of faith; 4. The Holy Spirit of God irresistibly draws sinners to Christ; 5. The chosen of God will never lose their eternal salvation.

Man falls according as God's providence ordains, but he falls by his own fault.
—JOHN CALVIN

CHRISTIA

NAE RELIGIONIS INSTI-
tutio, totam ferè pietatis summã, & quic
quid est in doctrina salutis cognitu ne-
cessarium, complectens : omnibus pietatis studiosis lectu dignissi-
mum opus, ac re
cens edi-
tum.

PRAEFATIO AD CHRI
stianißimum REGEM FRANCIAE, qua
hic ei liber pro confeßione fidei
offertur.

IOANNE CALVINO
Nouiodunensi autore.

BASILEAE,
M. D. XXXVI.

7

A Fateful Detour

When Calvin handed the finished manuscript of the *Institutes* to Thomas Platter, a publisher in Basel, on August 23, 1535, he wrote across the top of the page, "I am come not to send peace but a sword." This sword, however, would not be drawn in the city of Basel.

Toward the end of March 1536 Calvin and du Tillet mounted two horses in Basel and set off for Ferrara, Italy. Calvin had heard that Duchess Renée of Ferrara, a cousin of Marguerite of Angoulême, was a follower of the new Protestant movement. If any country needed to hear the gospel of faith, Calvin decided, it was Italy, the home of the pope. The men loaded their saddlebags with copies of the *Institutes*, which Platter had just finished printing, and set off across the Alps.

The journey took several weeks. The men passed over the Bernina Peak on a narrow trail through the Italian Alps. Soon they entered land that was dominated by the Catholic church; if anyone questioned

> *For Calvin the doctrine of election [predestination] was an unspeakable comfort because it eliminated the need to agonize for faith and freed man from concern about himself in order that he might devote every energy to the unflagging service of the sovereign Lord.*
> —ROLAND H. BAINTON
> American historian

Calvin, after completing his *Institutes*, traveled to Italy to attack the Catholic church on its home ground. However, when a royal amnesty was granted in France a few weeks later, he seized the opportunity to return to Noyon to see his family. Six months later he set out for Switzerland, finally leaving France forever.

> *It is not possible to serve God without a tranquil mind, for those who labor in inquietude, who dispute within themselves as to whether He is propitious or offended, whether He will accept or reject their prayers, those who in consequence wander between hope and fear and serve God anxiously can never submit themselves to Him sincerely and wholeheartedly.*
> —JOHN CALVIN

them they would have to disguise their true identities. Calvin, already a well-known author, assumed his usual alias, Charles d'Espeville. As the weary travelers saw the gold steeples of Ferrara in the distance, they disguised themselves as priests, hiding their breeches and doublets under clerical robes.

Calvin and du Tillet stayed with Duchess Renée for several weeks while she hid them from the threatening priests and cardinals in the court. Gradually, however, her husband, Duke Ercole II, grew suspicious of the court visitors. Wishing to avoid trouble, Calvin and du Tillet discontinued their work and made preparations to leave.

Du Tillet decided to travel to Geneva, where many Lutheran churches were taking root. Calvin, however, longed to see his homeland and family again. Francis I was still battling the Protestants, but the king had a new strategy. He thought if he guaranteed six months of freedom to the heretics they would return to France, realize their errors, and return to the Catholic church. Not realizing the French king's hidden motives, Calvin took advantage of the royal proclamation and returned to his half-sister Marie and his brother Antoine in Noyon.

The king's six-month promise soon came to an end in 1536 and the three siblings left for the free city of Strasbourg in Germany. Calvin was once again leaving his homeland, this time never to return to France.

Strasbourg lay just a short distance to the east of Paris. However, Holy Roman Emperor Charles V and King Francis I were once again at war. Traveling on the Campaigne Road to Strasbourg was stepping directly onto their battlefields. The three travelers had only gone a short distance when armored soldiers on horseback, brandishing lances and swords, shouted at them to turn back. They decided to take an alternative route by way of Geneva. Had Calvin known what lay in store for him there perhaps he would have chosen to cross the battlefield.

By the time Calvin, Marie, and Antoine passed the Cornavin Gate of Geneva, they could barely discern the details on the city's coat of arms on the sentry's box that guarded the city. On the base of the shield was stamped the motto: *Post Tenebras Lux* — After Darkness [is] Light. Perhaps it referred to the 30 years of fighting between Catholics and Protestants that had plagued the city. The Catholics were represented by the powerful bishop of Geneva and the dukes of Savoy, who owned castles that surrounded the city. The Protestants consisted of almost all of the city's citizenry, led by four magistrates or syndics. During this struggle William Farel, a zealous Protestant preacher, had emerged.

Of Farel, Erasmus was heard to have exclaimed, "Never in my life have I seen so bold a man." Farel often interrupted Catholic Masses by taking over the pulpit and preaching from the Bible. He gathered up relics being sold in the streets and threw them in the Rhine River. Wherever Farel went he was met with either protestors with swords or enthusiastic Lutheran followers.

Eventually, the dukes of Savoy gave Geneva an ultimatum: either it exile its Protestant preachers, specifically Farel, or they would attack the city. All

Geneva at the time of the Reformation was a fiercely independent city at the eastern edge of France. Its ruling bishop-prince was loyal to the French duke of Savoy, but the Genevan citizens were fighting for independence. Thanks to Calvin, the city would become known as "the Protestant Rome."

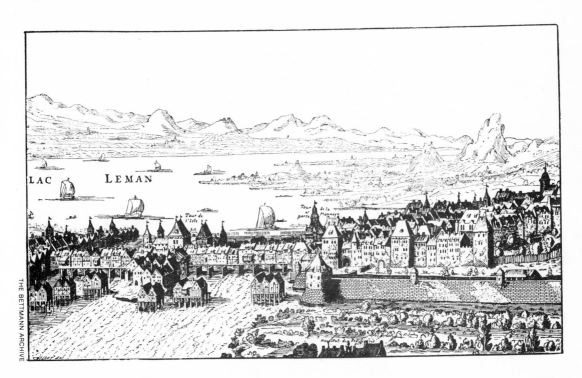

of Geneva gathered behind Farel. Protestants throughout the city destroyed Catholic altars and statues, converted monasteries to hospitals, and caused hundreds of monks, priests, and nuns to flee. The citizens of Geneva were willing to risk death rather than submit to the dukes and the Catholic church. They bravely supported the Protestant cause and united together to defeat the opposition in combat and to form a strong Lutheran church.

A new government was established. The bishop was permitted to remain in Geneva, but the city was now ruled by three councils: the Little Council, composed of four syndics; the Council of the Sixty; and the Council of the Two Hundred. All appointments were made according to the newly established constitution. In May 1536, the Genevan Councils issued an edict announcing that Rome's religion (Catholicism) was no longer their religion.

Soon after their successful battle for freedom the Genevans began to fight among themselves and forget the new fervor for the life of faith in God. The zealous Farel had begun to lose his impact; the people needed a trained pastor rather than a wild fanatic to guide them. Into this stormy situation rode Calvin. However, Calvin was only concerned with traveling to Strasbourg and partaking in the peaceful privacy that the German city had to offer for his studies. He planned to leave Geneva the following morning; someone else would have to worry about this city's church.

Calvin was abruptly awakened in the morning by a crazed man with darting eyes and a red beard. Hovering over his bed, screaming, was Farel. The preacher had read the *Institutes*, and he firmly believed that God himself had brought Calvin to heal his divided city. He commanded the reluctant Calvin to remain in Geneva. "I declare in the name of the almighty God that if you refuse to take part in the Lord's work in this church, God will curse the quiet life that you want for your studies!" he cried.

"I felt," said Calvin, "as if God from heaven had lain His mighty hand upon me to stop me in my course, and I was so stricken with terror that I did not continue my journey."

Protestant iconoclasts destroy a Catholic church in Geneva. The Genevans were determined to separate from France, and, to that end, they declared in 1535 that Catholicism was no longer the state religion. Calvin would be the inspiration and unifying force of the new Protestant faith there.

8

The City of Swords

Life was very difficult for Calvin in Geneva. He later wrote of his stay in the city, "Although it was a very troublesome province to me, the thought of deserting it never entered my mind. For I considered myself placed in that position by God, like a sentry at his post, from which it would be impiety on my part were I to move a single step. Yet I think you would hardly believe me were I to relate to you even a very small part of those annoyances, nay miseries, which we had to endure for a whole year. This I can truly testify, that not a day passed in which I did not long for death ten times over."

Calvin began his work in Geneva as a "professor of Sacred Letters," lecturing in St. Peter's Cathedral to a small congregation that came to hear his commentaries on the writings of the apostle Paul. Every evening he walked home down rue de la Treille, exhausted by his teaching and discouraged by his apparent ineffectiveness. All around him he saw drunkenness, gambling, prostitution, and crime. Calvin objected to the dancing in the public square, the immodest silks, jewels, and gaudy doublets of

Because the Papists persecute the truth should we on that account refrain from repressing error.
—JOHN CALVIN

Calvin soon became discouraged and angry with the citizens of Geneva. He wanted their whole lives to be lived in the spirit of God and his reformist teachings, but his strict rules for behavior and total lack of compassion for offenders outraged even his own government.

the people. In the seclusion of the cathedral the people heard the message of faith, but they were not living the teaching of Jesus in the streets of Geneva. For Calvin, it was not enough just to have faith; the

Calvin presents his treatise on the organization of the Genevan church to the Genevan Councils. They had begged him for a strong statement of faith, but Calvin made them accept a faith written into law, with strict religious and civil penalties.

believer must also be obedient to the teachings of the Word of God.

Calvin was convinced that he had to organize a strong church to discipline and guide the believers.

Luther, whose later career was in striking contrast to Calvin's. Whereas Calvin was intent on establishing a theocracy, or church-governed state, the German monk disliked being identified with either a church or a state government. "Call yourselves not Lutherans but Christians," Luther begged.

For Calvin, the church was "the mother of all who have God for their Father. There is no other way of entrance into life but by our being conceived by her. . . . We must continue under her instruction of discipline until the end of our lives." Calvin desired to achieve this strong "mother church" in Geneva, a church modeled after the New Testament, made up of every citizen in the city. It was to be a national church which determined the moral law of Geneva; the citizen's sinful ways could be monitored and punished by the governing church body. The Genevan Councils requested that a general statement of belief be presented as the basis for this new church. The distinguished Calvin was asked to compose the statement.

On November 10, 1536, Calvin presented a treatise based on his *Institutes* to the Genevan Councils, entitled *The Confession of Faith, which all the citizens and inhabitants of Geneva . . . must promise to keep and to hold.* Calvin demanded that everyone who failed to confess the faith outlined in his article must be excommunicated and cast into "the power of Satan, for he becomes an alien and is cast out of Christ's kingdom!"

Two months later, on January 16, 1537, Farel and Calvin presented to the councils another treatise, *Articles on the Organization of the Church and its Worship at Geneva.* The basic suggestions of this new presentation were not radical, but the implications and applications of the document caused much alarm.

The reformers addressed four basic issues in the *Articles*: the Lord's Supper, hymn singing, the education of children, and marriage. The main theme of the treatise, however, was the emphasis of a controlling church body. Their ideas concerning the legislation of the Lord's Supper were particularly alarming to the citizens and councils of Geneva. Calvin wanted to prevent those who were disobedient to the Gospel from participating in the Lord's Supper. He called for overseers in every part of the city — people who would report the sins of Christians to the ministers of the church. Were they seen with a prostitute? Did they miss a Sunday service?

> *The word hope I take for faith; and indeed hope is nothing else but the constancy of faith.*
> —JOHN CALVIN

Were they found playing cards in a tavern?

Calvin was relentlessly strict in insisting on a "holy" lifestyle based on obedience to the Word of God. Any deviance, if persistent, would eventually lead to excommunication. But the Genevans were not interested in Calvin's organizational plan. They had just narrowly escaped the rule of the dukes of Savoy; they demanded their freedom — moral and otherwise. The burghers, or prominent citizens, of Geneva refused to follow Calvin's orders, and the councils began to grow uneasy over his attempts to make the church independent of state controls.

Needless to say, Calvin was not a popular man in the city. Some wrote ballads against him, and someone even offered 500 crowns to the assassin who would kill him.

Calvin was a man who would not compromise. He would not retract one principle of his treatises. Compared to German reformer Martin Luther, whose humble, emotional sermons and writings converted thousands to the Protestant cause, Calvin was a cold, inflexible scholar of the Word. He rarely spoke of his own spiritual feelings or troubles; his was an austere faith that had little patience for sin or disbelief.

A well-known story illustrates Calvin's severity. One day at a dinner party in Geneva, a playing card manufacturer named Pierre Ameaux sat across from Calvin, laughing with the other guests. Ameaux's business had suffered since Calvin had come to Geneva. Having had a lot to drink, Ameaux became boisterous and denounced Calvin as a preacher of doctrines that were not those of the Bible. He also criticized Calvin's censorship, which he said should not be taken seriously. His remarks were quickly reported to the city councils and by the following morning Ameaux was a prisoner awaiting judgment.

Several days later the order came that the man was to kneel and ask for Calvin's forgiveness before the magistrates. Enraged at the leniency of the councils, Calvin insisted that only public humiliation would be sufficient. Calvin demanded that Ameaux crawl on his knees through the city streets

Calvin faced great danger as he preached on Easter morning, 1538, in the Church of the Rive. Offended by Calvin's fanaticism, Geneva's government refused to enact his rigid penalties, and finally barred him and his fellow preacher Farel from its pulpits. Defying the ban, Calvin was finally exiled from the city, to where he was sure he would never return.

in repentance, carrying a candle and begging for God's mercy.

Many Genevans were offended by Calvin's vehemence and rallied against him. "Take him to the river and drown him!" was their common cry. Some left the Protestant movement, blaming the youth and inexperience of Calvin; others left due to renewed contact with Catholics to the west and south. Even Calvin's old friend, Louis du Tillet, criticized the unswerving rules of the reformer.

According to Calvin it was "a most miserable situation." In February 1538, however, matters came to a head. The councils had signed the *Articles* of Calvin and Farel, but they refused to enforce Calvin's severe discipline. Furthermore, the government overrode Calvin's prescription for the Lord's Supper. Geneva would follow the church of Bern's more moderate procedures, not Calvin's. The politicians of Geneva needed Bern's support; if the preachers failed to comply they would be replaced.

Farel and Calvin both agreed that the church of Bern's doctrines were basically acceptable. The points that differed from their own document were insignificant. Should the bread be leavened or unleavened? Should the church use a baptismal font? But they could not condone the Genevan government's overruling of church authority. They would only accept Bern's methods if they conformed to the church constitution of Geneva. The city councils, however, wanted to govern the church as well as the city and required complete submission. The two reformers refused and the syndics passed the verdict — Calvin and Farel were banned from the pulpit.

On Easter morning, crowds pushed their way through the door of St. Peter's Cathedral, wondering whether Calvin would preach. Across the river, the church of St. Gervais was also overflowing with Protestants who were curious whether Farel would also defy the councils. The preachers arrived in a flurry of excited shouting. They boldly took their places behind the pulpits and preached as usual. That afternoon Calvin also preached in the Church of the Rive. In the middle of his sermon, a group of

THE BETTMANN ARCHIVE

William Farel, a zealous and impatient reformer, was a powerful preacher in Geneva. Convinced that God had sent Calvin to unite the Genevan Protestants, Farel threatened the French reformer with God's curse to persuade him to stay.

armed men brandishing swords jumped up on the altar. Friends of Calvin quickly shielded him and carried him to safety. "By a miracle," one man reported, "no one was killed." The Council of the Two Hundred immediately convened. On Monday they announced their decision — the two preachers were ordered into exile.

On April 25, 1538, Calvin and Farel passed the Cornavin Gate and the city's coat of arms. The motto on the shield was hardly visible by the time Calvin looked back over his shoulder. Calvin turned away from Geneva to face the long road ahead, and swore that he would rather die a thousand deaths before returning to the city. But Calvin's work in the troubled city of Geneva had only just begun.

9

The Welfare of the Church

Discouraged and angry, Calvin and Farel traveled back to the peaceful city of Basel to rest, study, and write. The 125-mile trip was treacherous. Due to torrential rains and melting snows the Rhine had grown to threatening proportions. Calvin later described the journey to his friend in Lausanne, "We have at length reached Basel, but well soaked with rain and completely spent and worn out. Nor was our journey free from perils, for in truth one of us was almost carried away by the swollen currents; but we have experienced more tender treatment from the impetuous river than from our fellow men!" In late May 1538 they arrived in Basel.

Farel soon decided to travel to the city of Neuchâtel, to which he had previously brought the teachings of Luther. Calvin, in turn, received a letter asking him to return to Strasbourg. The French Protestant refugees there needed a pastor. Calvin decided to join its 500-member congregation. For the next three years Calvin wrote and taught in Strasbourg. He also began to translate the *Institutes* into French and at the same time expanded it to

We are saved not by works, yet not without works.
—JOHN CALVIN

Title page to a book of psalms with a commentary by Calvin. His exile from Geneva gave him the peace and freedom that he had longed for. In Strasbourg, where he served as pastor to the French Protestant community, he could at last devote himself to writing, translating, and teaching. But his peace was to be short-lived.

three times its original length.

Compared to the miserable years in Geneva, Calvin's studious life in Strasbourg was happy. He worked closely with Martin Bucer, a popular teacher in the city. Calvin learned much about Bucer's doctrine of the church and pastoral care, including the duties of elders, pastors, teachers, and deacons. Bucer also had his own ideas concerning the meaning of predestination, and these greatly influenced young Calvin.

By September Calvin was settled in his home. Suddenly Calvin's good fortunes began to take a turn. Farel's nephew died of the plague. Courauld, a friend and colleague from Geneva, died in Orbe. And Calvin's good friend Olivétan was poisoned in the Italian court of Ferrara. To make matters worse, Louis du Tillet wrote Calvin a disturbing letter saying he had returned to the Catholic church, and insisted that Calvin's exile was a sign of God's displeasure. Heartbroken, Calvin replied, "It is to God that I appeal from the judgments of all worldly wise men who imagine their word carries enough weight to condemn us."

Over the years, from his many trials and labors, Calvin had grown progressively more irritable, and accepted criticism from neither du Tillet nor Bucer. Friends suggested that a wife might soften Calvin's hardening heart; Farel urged Calvin to send him a list of what he found most attractive in a woman. Calvin replied, "Always keep in mind what I seek to find in her; for I am not one of those insane lovers who embrace even the vices of those they are in love with when they are smitten at first sight with a fine figure. The only beauty which allures me is this — that she be chaste, not too nice or fastidious, economical, patient, likely to take care of my health."

Farel introduced many ladies to the reformer before Calvin finally chose Idelette de Bure. She was a widow of a Protestant and a mother of two children. Calvin was beside himself with joy. The two were married on August 10, 1540. Farel came from Neuchâtel to perform the ceremony, and Calvin's brother Antoine was the ringbearer. The bells of Strasbourg tolled in celebration of the betrothal.

Martin Bucer was a German Protestant who had a strong influence on the younger, more radical Calvin in Strasbourg. Bucer's aim was to make peace among the various Protestant reformers.

Since Calvin's exile confusion reigned in Geneva. The syndics and the councils were arguing among themselves; the church had almost disbanded; the Genevans were calling for the immediate return of the exiled reformers.

In the meantime, Calvin had traveled to Ratisbon (Regensburg, Germany) to hear Martin Luther debate several Catholic theologians. While at the Diet of Ratisbon, Calvin was approached by a delegation from the councils of Geneva. They begged him to return to their city. The thought of returning to that irreverent and faithless mob disturbed Calvin. He sent the delegation away unanswered. But thoughts of Geneva did not let him rest. In the spring of 1540

At the time of Calvin's stay in Strasbourg, it probably closely resembled this artist's impression. Though now French, the town was then a free city. The concentration of churches bears witness to the importance religion had to the citizens, and Calvin remained with his small congregation there for three years.

Calvin received an official invitation from the Genevan Councils: "Our good brother and special friend: we commend ourselves most affectionately to you. Because we know that you desire nothing but the increase and advancement of the glory and honor of God and his Holy Word, we ask you, on behalf of the Little, Grand, and General Councils, that you will move us and return to your former place and ministry. . . . Be assured that our people greatly desire you. We will treat you in such a way that you will have occasion to be pleased." Despite the Genevans' pleas, Calvin was extremely reluctant to return: "I would submit to death a hundred times rather than to that cross on which I had to daily suffer a thousand deaths."

Calvin sought advice from his friends and prayed for many weeks. Once again, Farel threatened Calvin with thunderbolts if he did not obey God's summons to Geneva. Calvin replied: "The thunderbolts which you so strangely hurl at me . . . have filled me with the greatest terror and dismay. You know that I have dreaded this summons, but that I have not been deaf to it." After several initial refusals, Calvin agreed to return to the city of swords, explaining that, "the welfare of this church, it is true, lay so near to my heart, that for its sake I would not have hesitated to lay down my life."

On September 13, 1541, Calvin arrived in Geneva for the second time. Antoine, Marie, his pregnant wife Idelette, and her two children went with him. Once more Calvin passed through the Cornavin Gate, a gate he at one time cursed. Upon his arrival, the councils paid him "twelve measures of corn and two tuns [504 gallons] of wine." But Calvin did not recommit himself to the troubled city for this slight salary from the government; his payment was in knowing that he was following the path that God had prepared for him.

The Strasbourg Council had only given Calvin a six-month leave of absence from his ministerial duties, but the rector would remain in Geneva for the next 23 years until his death. From 1541 to 1564 Calvin would be the most important leader of the Protestant Reformation.

> *Calvinism is a theory that might have been expected to sink men crouching and paralyzed into the blackest abysses of despair, and it has in fact been answerable for much anguish in many a human heart. Still it has proved itself a famous soil for rearing heroic natures. Founded on St. Paul and Augustine, Calvinism exalted its votaries to a pitch of heroic moral energy that has never been surpassed.*
> —JOHN MORLEY
> British historian

10

The Uncompromised Ideal

Calvin returned to Geneva on the condition that a "settled government" was established, "as is prescribed to us in the word of God, and such as was in use in the ancient Church." The syndics, eager for peace in the city, agreed, and Calvin began to compose his prescription for a New Testament church, which was to be established in Geneva.

Calvin recommenced with full force his work as a reformer. Meanwhile, his family moved into 11 rue des Chanoines, the home where Calvin would spend the rest of his life. The house was in the heart of Geneva. Down the hill from the building flowed the Rhine, which separated Geneva into two parts, St. Gervais and the city itself. The church of St. Gervais dominated one side; the cathedral of St. Peter filled the other bank with its glorious towers.

Calvin's family enjoyed their large but simple

> *Beyond the bosom of the [Protestant] Church no remission of sins is to be hoped for, nor any salvation.*
> —JOHN CALVIN

When Calvin returned to Geneva in 1541, it was with a new wife and family. The city, which had fallen into near anarchy after Calvin's expulsion, had promised him that its government would adopt and enforce his teachings. Since Calvin's time, Geneva has been identified with his austere, disciplinarian legacy.

Cain killing his brother Abel. Calvin's enemies in Geneva compared him to the Old Testament figure. Far more than a pun on Calvin's name, this comparison was an indictment of his harsh, tyrannical domination over the lives of the people.

home. Idelette's two children spent their summer days playing in the family's spacious garden, which sloped to meet the city wall in the back. From the bedroom upstairs the children could see the calm lake beyond the city, the Jura Mountains to the left, and the Alps to the right. Geneva, with its 13,000 inhabitants, welcomed its old friend with open arms, as it did the many travelers and merchants who passed through its ports.

Calvin suffered several terrible disappointments in his family life. His son Jacques, born prematurely, died in infancy in late July 1542. Three years later, Calvin and Idelette had a daughter who also died shortly after birth, and two years later a third child died at birth. In a letter to his friend Pierre Viret, Calvin wrote, "The Lord has certainly inflicted a severe and bitter wound in the death of our baby son. But He is Himself a father and knows best what is good for his children." Idelette was extremely weakened from the miscarriage and on March 29, 1549, she too died. Calvin wrote to his friend Viret the following week, "Truly mine is no ordinary . . . grief. I have been bereaved of the best companion of my life."

Although suffering with much bitter sadness, Calvin continued to work for reform. He wanted to put into practice all that he had formulated in his *Institutes*, and he hoped to bring the Bible and faith into the day-to-day lives of the Genevans: "He holds our life in His hands, He will take good and safe care of it; and what is more, He wants us to strain towards Him, that we may be content with knowing that He will not defraud us of what He promised to us." But Calvin also asked, "What will be the consequences if every man be at liberty to follow his own inclinations?" In order to experience God's blessings, the believer needed discipline and guidance from the church.

The Catholic church guided Christians through various rituals — confessions to priests, indulgences, offerings at shrines. To replace that discipline in the reformed church, Calvin drew up the *Ecclesiastical Ordinances*, which were signed into law by the councils on November 20, 1541. These

> *A denial of predestination meant banishment. A denial of immortality and the Trinity meant death. A fracas in the streets was interpreted as a coup against the state. Some of the opposition leaders were executed, some were banished. Thus, by the expulsion of dissenters and the inclusion of the conformists Geneva became a city of the saints.*
> —ROLAND H. BAINTON
> American historian, describing conditions in Geneva under Calvin's theocracy

Ordinances were articles that arranged both the affairs of the Genevan church and the general moral life of the city. Geneva became, in effect, a state run by the church — a theocracy. Calvin outlined four types of church officials — pastors, teachers, elders, and deacons — and described their qualifications and correct conduct. He also detailed such practices as the frequency, place, and time of preaching, the proper order of the service in church, visits to the sick, and the admonishment of those who failed to follow the *Ordinances*.

Some of the *Ordinances* addressed very specific offenses and reproofs: "No one shall invite another to drink . . .; taverns shall be closed during the sermon; anyone singing indecent, licentious songs, or dancing . . . shall be kept in prison three days and then sent to the councils." Calvin's regulations were responsible for sending citizens to prison if they so much as smiled at a baptismal service, broke a Sabbath law, or adorned themselves with unpermitted finery. In one instance a man was imprisoned for insisting that his son be named Claude instead of Abraham. Calvin's theocratic government became, as a contemporary stated, "an inquisitorial, harsh, tyrannical system of legally enforced obedience." Some of those who opposed Calvin's laws and doctrines were even executed.

The restrictions that the reformer imposed did not suit the people of Geneva. Anti-Calvin sentiments once again arose everywhere. At one point, renegades hung a poster on some corpses of the executed near Geneva that said, "Wanderer, reflect on the evil accomplished by Calvin. Who, deprived of L and V, presents himself as a second Cain [who killed his brother, Abel, in the book of Genesis]. Take out one L, which so imprudently flies. Take out one open V, by all the evil of Calvin, You know his violent rage. Knowing him, you judge him Cain." Despite the promises formerly made to Calvin that the councils and citizens would behave differently toward him if he returned, opposition was rampant. Calvin often complained of the conflicts, "I have been assailed on all sides, and have scarcely been able to enjoy repose for a single moment, but have always had to sustain some conflict either from enemies without or within the church."

Calvin had argued with many theologians over various doctrinal points. One theologian in particular, Sebastian Castellio, had provoked Calvin's anger when he called the Song of Songs (also known as the Song of Solomon) in the Bible "a lascivious and obscene poem." Calvin brought Castellio before the councils, challenging Castellio on several issues, including his interpretation of the Apostles' Creed. After a lengthy hearing, the magistrates promptly banished Castellio from Geneva, having judged his utterances slanderous. In the meantime, other Christians were actively dissenting. Finally, one incident occurred that brought the Genevan Reformation to a dangerous intensity.

Michael Servetus, a Spanish theologian and physician, did not agree with Calvin's orthodox concept of the Trinity — the triune Godhead of the Father, the Son, and the Holy Spirit — and published a book in 1553 attacking this notion. He also criticized the idea of original sin, a concept central to Calvinist doctrine, maintaining that a newborn infant, without knowledge of good and evil, could not be sinful. He also asserted that one may gain God's favor through faith and good works, thereby denying Calvin's notion of predestination. At Calvin's request, Servetus was arrested and imprisoned in Lyons, France. Calvin was called to the trial to prosecute the Spaniard. "I hope," Calvin wrote to the preacher Farel, "that a sentence of death will at last be passed upon him. . . ."

For months Servetus defended himself against Calvin's accusations. At last, after seeking the advice of other Swiss churches, the councils decided that Servetus would be burned at the stake as a heretic. Upon hearing his sentence, Servetus fell to his knees and begged for a death by the sword rather than by fire. The councils, however, would not hear his plea. On October 27, 1553, Servetus was tied to the stake and burned.

The Servetus affair brought on a wave of public indignation, for the reformed church was no longer merely excommunicating its dissenters, but, like

The origin of election consists of this: that the pure goodness of God made salvation available to us.
—JOHN CALVIN

Michael Servetus paid the ultimate price for opposition to Calvin's ideas. His more hopeful interpretation of the Scriptures was condemned as heresy, and in 1553 he was burned at the stake. Calvin's regime was now as repressive as the one in France under which he himself had suffered persecution.

THE BETTMANN ARCHIVE

the Catholic church, was routinely executing the opposition. One radical opposing party, the Libertines, composed mainly of aristocrats from a prominent Genevan family, had vehemently opposed Calvin for many years. When they tried to use the Servetus case to discredit Calvin, the Libertine leaders were quickly condemned to death. Though the leaders fled Geneva, avoiding death at the stake, some of the lesser party members were executed, and the Libertine opposition was quickly silenced.

Despite the recent tragedies, Calvin still held a position of tremendous power, and Geneva became a model Protestant city. In 1556 the Scottish reformer John Knox exclaimed, "Here exists the most perfect school of Christ that ever was on the earth since the days of the Apostles." Lang, a German historian, explained that "Geneva, saturated with the piety of Calvin, became the spring from which Calvinism in its extraordinarily vigorous expansion in all the countries of Europe ever drew new strength. . . . The ideal, embodied in Geneva, inspired [martyrs] to hold out until death."

But through the many years of desperate struggle, unending study, and regimens of preaching and lecturing twice a week, Calvin's health began to fail him. He had always had a frail constitution, but as a man in his early 40s, his thin, stooped body made him look almost twice his age.

John Knox was a great admirer of Calvin's reforms. Calling Calvin's Geneva "the most perfect school of Christ," the stern Scottish preacher came to Geneva in 1554 to minister to the English Protestant exiles. Soon Scotland would become a Calvinist country under Knox's leadership.

THE
Historie of the
REFORMATION
of the
CHURCH of ENGLAND

SUPERSTITION

RELIGION

THE HOLY BIBLE

THE POPE

SUPREMACY

PIPES

DECREES

LONDON
Printed for Ric: Chiswell

R. White Sculpsit

11

The Institution of Calvin

After the defeat of the Libertines in 1555, Geneva truly became the "cité calviniste." The law of God was the law of the land. Calvin, knowing that he was in his last years, decided to begin his own university to ensure that his work would continue even after his death. He collected donations from Geneva's citizens and asked noted scholars from all over Europe to teach with him in the city. Many sympathetic professors from Bern joined him (the councils of Bern had been hostile to Calvin's followers for many years). Calvin also invited his old Latin teacher from the Collège de la Marche, Mathurin Cordier, to take a place at the new school.

On March 5, 1559, the faculty gathered at St. Peter's Cathedral to celebrate the opening of the Academy of Geneva. Above its doors was chiseled, "The fear of the Lord is the beginning of wisdom." Calvinism had become an institution.

Calvin had changed none of his original doctrines of 1536. He still maintained his basic beliefs in the sovereignty of God, predestination, providence, and justification by faith. Neither had he changed his

I am certain that what I have taught and written did not grow in my brain, but that I hold it from God.
—JOHN CALVIN

Title page for a history of the English Reformation. King Henry VIII, founder of the Anglican church, is shown with a Protestant priest. Calvin's ideas were adopted by the English Puritans, and taken by them to New England in the early 17th century.

THE BETTMANN ARCHIVE

As Calvin lay on his deathbed, he continued to work for his ideals. His funeral would be as stark and simple as his life had been. Many churches followed his example, but in no place besides Geneva would his rules be so enshrined in law.

political or sociological theories concerning the role of church and state. In Geneva, he had lived to see

The 1572 St. Bartholomew's Day Massacre in Paris claimed the lives of an estimated 50,000 Huguenots. These French followers of Calvin had formed many of their own churches. They continued violent wars with French Catholics for decades after Calvin's death and through future generations. Not until the French Revolution in 1789 was religious freedom finally guaranteed in France.

the principles of the *Institutes* at work in the ordering of the church and in the lives of the people.

On Christmas Day, 1559, the Genevan Councils met in the city hall to award Calvin an honorary citizenship. The recognition was belated, but nevertheless timely. On that day, while returning from the hall, Calvin collapsed. Weakened from years of little sleep and constant labor, Calvin had contracted what would now be diagnosed as tuberculosis. Even sickness could not keep him from his labors. He continued to work on his *Institutes*, lecturing, and writing commentaries. Calvin would endure almost another four years, preaching his last sermon on February 6, 1564, barely able to stand.

John Calvin died on May 27, 1564. He left very specific instructions for his funeral, wishes that reflected the austerity and discipline of his character. His body was to be wrapped in a simple white cloth and enclosed in a bare, pine coffin. He wanted neither singing nor sermons at his grave. Hundreds of mourning followers, however, walked behind the coffin to the city's common cemetery of Plain-palais.

Calvin's will bespeaks a humble man who spent his entire life in service to God: "I confess to live and die in this faith which He has given me, inasmuch as I have no other hope or refuge than His predestination upon which my entire salvation is grounded. . . . Moreover, I declare that I endeavored to teach His Word undefiled and to expound Holy Scripture faithfully according to the measure of grace which He has given me. . . . But, oh, my will, my zeal were so cold and sluggish that I know myself guilty in every respect; without His infinite goodness, all my passionate striving would only be smoke."

Calvin's impact on the whole of Europe is inestimable. The Frenchman never returned to live in his native land, but his teachings had a lasting influence in France as elsewhere. By 1559, 72 Calvinist churches were established in France. A Catholic ambassador from Venice, Italy, reported the following from France in 1561: "There is not one single province uncontaminated. Indeed in some provinces, such as Normandy, almost the whole of Brittany, Touraine, Poitou, Gascony, and a great part of Languedoc, of Dauphiny, and of Provence, com-

The Swiss reformer Theodore Beza was a pupil of Calvin. He continued the work Calvin had begun, spreading Calvin's message and influence throughout Switzerland. He also helped to publish the first Bible containing chapter and verse numbers.

prising three-fourths of the kingdom, congregations and meetings are held; and in these assemblies they read and preach, according to the rites and uses of Geneva. . . . Your Serenity [the pope] will hardly believe the influence and great power which the principal minister of Geneva, by name Calvin, a Frenchman, and a native of Picardy, possesses in this kingdom." The Huguenots, as these French Protestants were called, were less rigid than the Calvinists in Geneva, partly because the Catholic government of France did not impose the strict order of the *Ordinances* as did the Genevan Councils.

Calvinism spread to the north; eventually two-thirds of the Dutch Republic became Calvinist. Scotland was soon to become thoroughly Calvinist under the direction of the reformer John Knox. The Church of England at the end of Edward VI's reign, in its "Forty-Two Articles" incorporated Calvin's ideas of the Lord's Supper, free will, and predestination into the official doctrines of the Anglican church. In England, the teachings of Calvin also led to the creation of the Puritan sect, a term first used in the Church of England in 1564, denoting a group of Christians wishing to "purify" the Anglican church by returning to the basic precepts of the Bible. The English Puritans of the 17th century eventually settled in the colonies in America, forming the basis of Puritanism in New England.

Calvin's work as a Swiss reformer was continued by his pupil Theodore Beza, who extolled his mentor: "He lived 54 years, 10 months, 17 days, the half of which he spent in the ministry. . . . No theologian of this period wrote more purely, weightily, and judiciously, though he wrote more than any individual either in our recollection or that of our fathers."

Institutes of the Christian Religion and the strong body of the Calvinist church remain Calvin's greatest legacy. Yet we cannot forget the man himself — student, preacher, husband, father, political and social reformer, follower of God, and leader of countries. Calvin's epitaph captured the motivating force of his life: *"Soli Deo gloria"* — "To God alone the glory."

Farel, Calvin, Beza, and Knox (left to right) are seen in this detail from the Reformation Monument, Geneva. The cornerstone of this huge sculpture was laid on Calvin's 400th birthday on July 10, 1909. Calvin's statue stands facing the University of Geneva, the modern-day successor to his own academy.

Further Reading

Bainton, Roland H. *The Reformation of the Sixteenth Century*. Boston, Massachusetts: Beacon Press, 1985.

Beza, Theodore. *The Life of John Calvin*, tr. Henry Beveridge. Philadelphia, Pennsylvania: The Westminster Press, 1909.

Breen, Quirinus. *John Calvin: A Study in French Humanism*. Hamden, Connecticut: Archon Books, 1968.

Calvin, John. *Calvin's Calvinism*, tr. Henry Beveridge. Grand Rapids, Michigan: Wm. B. Eerdmans Publishing Company, 1950.

———. *A Compend of the Institutes of the Christian Religion*, ed. Hugh T. Kerr. Philadelphia, Pennsylvania: The Westminster Press, 1964.

Dakin, A. *Calvinism*. Philadelphia, Pennsylvania: The Westminster Press, 1946.

Dowey, E. A. *The Knowledge of God in Calvin's Theology*. New York: Columbia University Press, 1952.

McNeill, John T. *The History and Character of Calvinism*. New York: Oxford University Press, 1954.

Parker, T. H. L. *John Calvin: A Biography*. London: J. M. Dent and Son Ltd., 1975.

Spitz, Lewis W. *The Protestant Reformation: 1517–1559*. New York: Harper & Row Publishers, 1985.

Chronology

July 10, 1509	Born Jean Cauvin in Noyon, France
Oct. 31, 1517	According to legend, Martin Luther posts 95 theses to door of Wittenberg Castle church, attacking central precepts of Catholicism
May 21, 1521	Calvin receives a benefice as chaplain of a small chapel in Noyon
Aug. 1523	Begins study at the Collège de la Marche of the University of Paris
1526	Transfers to the Collège de Montaigu
1528	Receives master of arts
1528–29	Studies law in Orléans and Bourges
May 26, 1531	His father, Gérard Cauvin, dies in Noyon
1532	Calvin publishes his first book, a Latin commentary on Seneca's *De clementia*
Nov. 1533	A sermon Calvin co-wrote with Sorbonne rector Nicolaus Cop is condemned as heresy by the university faculty Calvin flees Paris and takes refuge in Angoulême
May–Sept. 1534	Imprisoned in Noyon after resigning his benefice
Oct. 1534	After Protestants paper French cities with anti-Catholic posters, King Francis I conducts campaign of persecution Calvin again flees Paris, this time to Basel, Switzerland
1536	The first edition of Calvin's seminal work, the *Institutes of the Christian Religion*, is published in Basel Calvin accepts an invitation from pastor William Farel to aid the reform movement in Geneva, Switzerland
Nov. 10, 1536	Presents his treatise *The Confession of Faith* to the Genevan Councils, outlining a system of beliefs for his proposed New Testament church
Jan. 16, 1537	Presents another treatise, *Articles on the Organization of the Church*, detailing his plan for a new church structure
April 25, 1538	Farel and Calvin banished from Geneva after defying a council order not to preach
1538–41	Calvin in exile in Strasbourg
Aug. 10, 1540	Marries Idelette de Bure in Strasbourg
Sept. 13, 1541	Returns to Geneva, where he remains for the rest of his life, establishing a model Protestant community
Nov. 20, 1541	Genevan Councils sign into law Calvin's *Ecclesiastical Ordinances*, which include his blueprint for church organization and his code for moral behavior
Oct. 27, 1553	At Calvin's urging, Michael Servetus is burned at the stake for publishing heretical commentaries on the Trinity
March 5, 1559	Calvin founds the Academy of Geneva
May 27, 1564	Dies, aged 65, in Geneva

Index

Sally Stepanek, a graduate of Yale University, is a free-lance writer and editor living in New York. She is also the author of *Martin Luther*, and *Mary, Queen of Scots* in the Chelsea House series WORLD LEADERS PAST & PRESENT.

Arthur M. Schlesinger, jr., taught history at Harvard for many years and is currently Albert Schweitzer Professor of the Humanities at City University of New York. He is the author of numerous highly praised works in American history and has twice been awarded the Pulitzer Prize. He served in the White House as special assistant to Presidents Kennedy and Johnson.